The Miracle of Music

The Miracle of Music

By Romel Joseph

Experience how Romel Joseph has used his musical knowledge and talent to overcome some of his most challenging life obstacles.

All proceeds from the purchase of this book will be used to build the Haiti Performing Arts Center, a long time dream of Romel Joseph, which will be his legacy to his beloved country of Haiti.

Published by:
Friends of Music Education for Haiti Inc.

Friends of Music Education for Haiti Inc.
www.friendsofmusiceducationforhaiti.org

ISBN: 978-0-9769847-0-2

Library of Congress Control Number: 250995

FMEH logo is the trademark belonging to Friends of Music Education for Haiti Inc.

PRINTED IN THE UNITED STATES OF AMERICA

I am dedicating this book to my two wonderful children: Victoria and Bradley Joseph, as well as to my ex-wife, Sherry Joseph-Dutton, who have been extremely supportive to me during my journey in life.

I also want to dedicate *The Miracle of Music* to my great friend, Onickel Augustin, without whom I would not have survived the earthquake experience, as well as my unreservedly supportive friends: Cecilia Harris Johnson, who has been a true inspiration and motivating force to me for the past thirty years, Archange Michel for his constant helpful advice, Jolius Tinhhomme, whom I have known since I was a child and is always there for me, all my employees at the New Victorian School, particularly Marcel and Boss Sonson, as well as Veriole, who were instrumental in getting me out from under the rubble following the earthquake of January 12th, 2010.

I also dedicate this book to the memory of Mr. Jack Seighman, Sherry's father and my former father-in-law who passed away this evening, August 24th, 2010. He was truly a special man, and I will always remember him for his uninhibited support to Sherry and me during our marriage. May his soul rest in peace.

Finally, I am dedicating this book to the memory of my late wife, Myslie Chery Joseph, and our unborn son, who died on her bed on January 12th 2010, during the earthquake. She was a unique and special woman, who at age twenty-six, died prematurely when she finally was going to enjoy what life had to offer her. May her soul rest forever in peace.

Acknowledgements

I would like to take the opportunity to thank everyone who has supported me through prayers, words of encouragement through phone calls, e-mail, frequent hospital visits, and the like during one of the most difficult times of my life: the days and months following the January 12th, 2010 earthquake. My special thanks also goes to all those who have made it financially possible to start the reconstruction of The New Victorian School, as well as their in-kind donations, such as musical instruments and other school materials. I will forever be grateful to you all.

Preface

I am writing this book in order to share with all of you my life story; the happy and unhappy times, the challenges I faced since my childhood, how I have managed to overcome many of them, the way in which I deal with life's successes or failures, and most importantly, how much God has done for me and how great He is. Nothing is impossible to God, and if you have faith in Jesus Christ, you can achieve anything. I hope reading this book will provide you with a few hours of introspection and fulfillment.

Table of Contents

Introduction

On January 12th, 2010, at 4:53 p.m., a 7.0 magnitude earthquake struck Haiti, and lasted for about thirty-five seconds. The epicenter, on a fairly shallow strike-slip fault, was eight miles deep and sixteen miles west of the capital, Port-au-Prince, and its 2.5 million inhabitants.

According to the US Geological Survey, this was Haiti's most violent quake in a century. Still-incomplete estimates suggest that almost 230,000 people died (or one in ten), and 300,000 were hurt. Corpses, the injured, and destruction littered the streets.

The quake left about one million inhabitants homeless when 250,000 residences and 30,000 commercial buildings collapsed, pancaked, or were severely damaged, including the Presidential Palace, the National Assembly Building, the Port-au-Prince Cathedral, the main prison, eleven government ministries, and 90 % of all schools and churches. Overall, three million citizens were affected, and the shock waves traveled as far as Cuba and Venezuela.

By January 24th, 2010, fifty-two major aftershocks had occurred, ranging in magnitude from 4.2 to 5.9, causing continued devastation and fear. By April, the rainy season had come, inundating vast tent cities and mass graves.

According to the PBS program *Frontline*, fewer than 150 people buried in the citywide rubble emerged alive. Of those, I was one of the selected few. I was trapped for eighteen hours in what I called my "little tomb" under the demolished five-story school I founded, but miraculously I survived with Jesus's presence, the assistance of some of my friends and employees, and especially by performing a different violin concerto or sonata every hour, in my head.

My name is Romel Joseph. I am Haiti's pre-eminent violin virtuoso. My life mission is to change lives by making classical music and learning a musical instrument available and accessible to all children.

Music, in its essence, is a miracle; that's why God used music during six days to create the world as well as accomplishing some of his other important works.

Since the beginning of time, music has been God's most useful tool in executing his tasks. For example, When God said, "Let there be light," he very likely said these words with certain rhythm -- each word had a certain length, the sentence was said with a specific speed, probably putting more emphasis on certain words than others; possibly some words were said louder than others, or all of them at the same dynamic level and using perhaps the same or different pitch for each words. In addition, we saw how God destroyed the wall of Jericho by using music in an orderly and systematic manner, thus using most of the characteristics of musical creation.

Consequently, if God -- who is omnipotent and omniscient -- finds music to be indispensible for the success of his work, why not give our children a chance to grow up with the proper musical training in order that they may use such knowledge to improve their lives based on their talents, intelligence and creativity?

Sister Joan, the director and founder of St. Vincent's School for Handicapped Children, where I grew up, did all that was possible so we all had musical training. She had all the instruments and teachers that she could find available to us, and we took full advantage of her wisdom. In this book, I will share with you how I was able to use music to overcome some of the most difficult challenges of my life, including surviving for eighteen hours locked within my little tomb.

1

My Early Childhood, (1959-1970.) St Vincent's School, Inferiority Complex, Cruelty, Survival.

I was born in Gros Mornes, Gonaives, Haiti, where my family resided, on May 19th, 1959, at 9:00 a.m. Gros Mornes is a small village in the center of northwestern Haiti with four main streets – which were not even paved when I came along. To find Gros Mornes, you have to look south and a little east of Port-de-Paix and quite a bit southwest of Cap Haitien – both of which are on the country's north coast. The village sits between the Les Trois Rivières (The Grand Rivière), where we would bathe and do the laundry, and the Rivières Marcelle, which is nasty and always dirty, especially when it rains. Gros Mornes hardly stands out on a map, except that highways 150 and 116 now meet there. About forty-five kilometers south is the port city of Gonaïves, Cité de l'Indépendance (nicknamed the Independence City) on the west coast, and 171 km further south is Port-au-Prince.

My first challenge: being virtually blind since childhood from an incurable eye infection. I lost my left eye completely at four years old, and I am so severely nearsighted in my right eye that while able to sense dark and light, colors, and general shapes, I am not able to see details. In other words, I can't distinguish faces and, more telling, I can't read sheet music unless it is inches from my face, and I have to wear special glasses. Consequently, I have to memorize all that I read.

I was born in a period under the regime of the President François Duvalier, where life in Haiti, particularly the political, social, and economic life was in turmoil. Duvalier, whatever one may think of him, would change the social fabric of Haiti forever.

François Duvalier was born on April 14th, 1907, and died on April 21st, 1971. He was the President of Haiti from 1957 until his death in 1971. He was the son of Duval Duvalier, a justice of the peace, and Ulyssia Abraham, a baker. Duvalier first won acclaim in fighting diseases, earning him the nickname "Papa Doc."

In 1946, Duvalier aligned himself with President Dumarsais Estimé, who my mother told me was loved by almost everyone, and Duvalier was appointed Director General of the National Public Health Service. In 1949, Duvalier served as Minister of both Health and Labor, but when General Paul Magloire ousted President Estimé in a coup d'état, Duvalier left the government and was forced into hiding until amnesty was declared in 1956.

In December of the same year, President Magloire resigned and left Haiti to be ruled by a succession of provisional governments. Then on September 22nd, 1957, presidential elections pitted Louis Déjoie, a mulatto landowner and industrialist from the north of Haiti, against Duvalier, who was backed by the military.

Duvalier campaigned as a populist leader, using a *noiriste* strategy of challenging the mulatto elite and appealing to the Afro-

Haitian majority. He described his opponent as part of the ruling mulatto class that was making life difficult for the country's rural black majority.

I wasn't alive to really know how bad it was. However, I was told by many who were around, that until the Duvalier presidency, black people were not allowed to walk around Turgeau after 6:00 p.m. , where The New Victorian School is located today. You would be arrested if you were found.

In addition, black people were not allowed to go to certain schools, like "Sainte Rose de Lima" a parochial school which we know today as "Mère Lalue" because the school is located on one of the main streets of Port-au-Prince name "Lalue."

The racial discrimination was extremely bad during the time Duvalier became president in 1959. By the time I was growing up, apparently the level of racism had abated to a point that most of us from the 1970s didn't even notice. Though his methods may have been ruthless, Duvalier brought about more racial equality and balance under his reign than those before him.

The election resulted in Duvalier defeating Déjoie with 678,860 votes. Déjoie polled 264,830 votes, and independent candidate Jumelle won a minor percentage of the electorate. Duvalier's only opponent among the black proletarians, Daniel Fignole, had been forcibly exiled before election, thus leaving Duvalier a path for a landslide.

After being sworn in on October 22nd, Duvalier exiled most of the major supporters of Déjoie, and had a new constitution adopted in 1957. He also changed the color of the flag from red and blue to red and black; which I think is more beautiful. As the late Haitian artist, Ansy Dérose, so nicely and poetically said in one of his songs: "Du rouge de notre sang, et du noir de notre peau." This is translated as: "The redness of our blood, and the darkness of our skin."

President Duvalier promoted and patronized members of the black majority in the civil service and the army. Yet in mid-1958, the army, which had supported Duvalier earlier, tried to oust him in another coup but failed. In response, Duvalier replaced the chief of staff with a more reliable officer and then proceeded to create his own power base within the army by turning the army's Presidential Guard into an elite corps aimed at maintaining Duvalier's power. After this, Duvalier dismissed the entire general staff and replaced it with officers owing their positions and their loyalty to him.

In 1958, three exiled Haitians and five Americans invaded Haiti and tried to overthrow Duvalier; all of them were killed. In 1959, the year I was born, Duvalier also created a rural militia, the *Milice Volontaires de la Sécurité Nationale* (MVSN, in English: *National Security Volunteer Militia*), commonly referred to as the "Tonton Macoutes," after a Creole term for the boogeyman, to extend and bolster support for the regime in the countryside. The *Macoutes*, which by 1961 had twice the number of soldiers as the regular army, never developed into a real military force, but were a mere secret police.

Based on my understanding, at first a Tonton Macoute referred to a violent person, faithful to the Duvalier regime. But eventually the term become synonymous with anyone who worked for the regime and said anything positive about it. Consequently, most black Haitians had become Tonton Macoutes, which was a dangerously life- threatening or fatal situation, as was the case for many innocent Haitians in 1986, when Jean Claude Duvalier left for Europe.

Sadly, I lost two of my best friends due to this situation:

THE MIRACLE OF MUSIC

Amérique, a multi-talented musician who was a pianist, violinist, violist, and keyboard player with whom I had grown up since age five; and Ti Pierre, who was, like Onickel, a role model for me in terms of music. He played violin, viola, piano, keyboard, guitar, drums, and electric bass. He was one of the greatest Haitian musicians of the 20th century.

Both of them, who were so savagely murdered, were totally blind, and on January 27th 1991, while we were rehearsing for the first of many concerts which were to take place through out 1991, in commemoration of 200th anniversary of Mozart's death, were burned alive because they were accused by former President Aristide fans (named "lavalasses") of being Tonton Macoute musicians. Ironically, Ti Pierre and Amérique were the two most nonpolitical people I have ever known in my life.

On May 24th, 1959, Duvalier suffered a massive heart attack, possibly as a result of an insulin overdose; he had been a diabetic since early adulthood and also suffered from heart disease and associated circulatory problems. During this heart attack, he was unconscious for nine hours; many associates believed that he suffered neurological damage which affected his mental health and made him paranoid.

While recovering, Duvalier left power in the hands of Clement Barbot, leader of the Tonton Macoutes. Upon his return, Duvalier accused Barbot of trying to supplant him as president and had him imprisoned. In April 1963, Barbot was released and began plotting to remove Duvalier from office by kidnapping his children. The plot failed and Duvalier subsequently ordered a massive search for Barbot and his fellow conspirators. During the search, Duvalier was told that Barbot had transformed himself into a black dog; consequently, Duvalier ordered that all black dogs in Haiti be put to death. Barbot was later captured and shot by the Tonton Macoutes in July 1963.

Duvalier's government was accused of being one of the most repressive in the hemisphere. Within the country, Duvalier apparently used both political murder and expulsion to suppress his opponents; estimates of those killed are as high as 30,000.

Of course, children like me didn't know anything about these crimes. At home, I remembered the curfews because I couldn't go to the bathroom, which was outside in my yard. I frequently heard my mother and father talking about the political situation, but I wasn't able to understand much because I was too young. Except one day, I remember my father being very sick. My father used to work for the government as "receveur communale" -- I guess that means he was like an accountant, because he was responsible for paying many government employees in Gros Mornes.

He was called to go to war in the northwestern part of Haiti to fight the Camokin. Camokin referred to the people who were fighting the Duvalier regime. According to my mother, my uncle, Benoit Joseph, who was also my godfather, was a mystic, and he didn't want to see his brother coming back from war in a body bag. So he gave my father a leaf which he was to insert inside of his anus. As soon as he did that, he started to suffer from violent hemorrhoids and was declared unfit for war. Then my uncle gave him another leaf which healed the hemorrhoids.

In terms of social and economic policies, Duvalier employed intimidation, repression, and patronage to supplant the old mulatto elite with a new elite of his own making. Corruption — in the form of government rake-offs of industries, bribery, extortion of domestic businesses, and stolen government funds — enriched the dictator's closest supporters. Most of these supporters held sufficient power to enable them to intimidate the members of the old elite, who were gradually co-opted or eliminated. Interestingly enough, François Duvalier didn't appear to die a rich man.

Educated professionals fled Haiti to reside in places such as Boston, New York City, French-speaking Montreal, Chicago, New Jersey, and several French-speaking African countries, exacerbating an already serious lack of doctors and teachers. Some of the highly skilled professionals joined the ranks of several UN agencies to work in development in newly independent nations such as Ivory Coast, and Congo. Many people believe that the country has never recovered from this brain drain.

The government confiscated peasant land holdings to be allotted to members of the militia who had no official salary and made their living through crime and extortion. The dispossessed swelled the slums by fleeing to the capital to seek meager incomes to feed themselves. Malnutrition and famine became endemic. Most of the aid money given to Haiti was spent improperly.

Nonetheless, Duvalier enjoyed significant support among Haiti's majority black rural population, who saw in him a champion of their claims against the historically dominant mulatto élite. During his fourteen years in power, he created a substantial black middle class, chiefly through government patronage. This large, well-educated black middle class left Haiti between 1979 and 1990, and is now residing mostly in the United States and Canada.

Duvalier also initiated the development of Mais Gate Airport, which was originally known as François Duvalier airport, and more recently as Toussaint L'Ouverture International Airport.

As children, we didn't know anything about all that. In Gros

Mornes, my father had a garden where I used to go every day. It had lots of mangoes, corn, bananas, and other plants. To my knowledge, we had no food problems. The country, though very poor, was highly decentralized. Few people lived in Port-au-Prince. The now new super-populated areas, such as Carrefour, Delmas, Tabarre, and Croix des Bouquets, were nothing but empty lands full of water and trees.

Though we didn't have electricity, cell phone, TV, or Internet, we had a radio. However, in the evening, our parents and elders would gather us together and tell us old traditional Haitian stories; such as the famous magic orange tree.

At St. Vincent's School, we were also sheltered from the horrible political or economic situation. In fact, from all I have heard from those older than me, including Sister Joan, Duvalier had great respect for St.Vincent's School, and did give it all the necessary protection and assistance except in 1963, when the life of Jean Claude Duvalier was in danger while he was in school in College Bird, a Methodist church/school almost across from the boys' dorm where I came to live in 1964.

In addition, many of the public schools had music education and were excellent. To our knowledge, Port-au-Prince didn't have all these children all over the streets cleaning cars. Any child that was found on the street was picked up by a group called Chalant, which would take the child home or to school. The prices of food, medical supplies, and other goods were regulated. The only thing I feared other than the Tonton Macoute was evil spirits; who would try to eat children, especially at night.

I am the fourth of six children; five of us survived. My father died in 1983, and my mother in 2005. My sister, Gilberte, is the oldest. She has her own school in Port-au-Prince -- but she slept through the earthquake unharmed. Harry, the third, is a journalist, living in the Dominican Republic, with his own radio show called Haiti Focus. After me came Herbert, who teaches in the New York City public schools, and my baby brother, Jean-Maret, who, like Gilberte and me, has his own school in Port-au-Prince. He's the brother who was buried for six hours when his school went down, then went to a hospital in Broward County, Florida, and then to New York, where his health is steadily getting better. The earthquake took away his wife and two children.

My older brother, Vanelle, died when he was three months old. According to the folk stories, any time a child is born in Haiti, evil spirits want to eat the child. There are many spirits, both in the Voudu (Voodoo in English) tradition and outside, like the loup-garou, a person who can change himself into an animal -- in this case, a wolf.

My mother, Carmèlite, told me that when I was born, a swarm of lightning bugs surrounded her. She saw this as an omen that the spirits also wanted to "eat" me, but couldn't. Instead, they left me with poor eyesight.

The spirits are everywhere. My mother once told me that she was six months pregnant with Herbert before she realized it. It took a Vodou priest to convince her she was, by giving her some medicine that suddenly made her stomach huge. Everyone went, "Wow, you're pregnant." According to her, the baby was tied in her back and she would have died. I know it sounds weird, but these are the stories I've always heard.

For as far back as I can remember, music was my life. As a child, I spent much of my time listening to "4 VEH," a wonderful Christian radio station, every morning from 5:00 a.m. to 8:00 a.m., and afternoons from 2:00 p.m. to 3:00 p.m., and memorized some of the most popular Christian songs of the time. I also learned about traditional Haitian music, mostly when I went to Grand Rivière with my mother and sister. The ladies who were washing their clothes would be singing all kind of beautiful songs.

I also was facinated with conpas, which has been the most popular dancing music for Haitians for the past fifty years. I would listen to compas on other radio stations, particularly on Radio Haiti, Radio Caraibes, Radio Port-au-Prince (which no longer exists), and Radio MBC. Also, my father played the trumpet. I often heard him practice, and he belonged to the hometown fanfare, which was the local band.

I don't think Voudu spirits had anything to do with my very poor eyesight. I had an infection, from birth, that would never go away, and so my visual memories of childhood are rare and by now mostly forgotten. During the first four years of my life, my mother frequently took me to the Hospital Albert Schweitzer in Desjardines/Deschapelles, where they put medicine in my eyes. Founded by Dr. William Larimer Mellon and Gwen Grant Mellon in 1956, today the hospital provides care and community health for over 300,000 poor in the neglected rural Artibonite Valley of Central Haiti.

The trip was almost 100 kilometers one way, and exhausting. Even worse, it would be an all-day affair and many times the "zobopes," or the "bizangoes," and the "champrel"-- which are all different types of evil groups -- would try to eat us even in daylight.

There at the hospital, the doctors would tie my hands to keep me from touching my eyes, because the medicine burned. I remember once at 4 years old, negotiating with a nurse, saying, "If you untie my hands, I won't touch my eyes. I promise." To my surprise, she untied me, so I didn't touch them. I suppose that even very early I had good self- control. Unfortunately the medicine didn't work and Doctor Gerard Frederique, who remained my ophthalmologist for years, had to remove my left eye when I was four. My right eye could still distinguish dark from light and see very fuzzy shapes, but I was declared legally blind. Years later, Doctor Rowe, an ophtomologist, in Cincinnati, Ohio, where I went to college at the Conservatory of Music, removed a massive cataract from my right eye and wondered why it hadn't been repaired when I was younger. He said that since very little light had been able to penetrate the cataract, my retina had been permanently weakened.

Just before he died, I asked Dr. Frederique if he could explain. He said he'd worried that operating on my "good" eye when I was only four risked causing total blindness — a worse choice. I guess I could be angry, but what's the point? Whatever happened to me, happened. My parents took care of my eye situation the best way they could and that's all I know.

My mother was a seamstress who took in work. She also taught young women how to cook. At the time, Haitian parents didn't believe that women should go to high school or to college. Heaven forbid. After the equivalent of the American sixth grade, they'd send the girls to vocational school for a number of years, to learn everything they needed to know about how to be useful to a husband. It wasn't a matter of her being happy or unhappy with the situation. Most women got married between the ages of eighteen and twenty anyway; that's just how it was in Haitian society, which was pretty chauvinist.

My father was a tailor. Since we had no shops nearby where

you could buy clothes, they had to be made. Gros Mornes was so small that we didn't have many shops at all. Instead, we relied on farmers from the surrounding area who would come on every Monday, Wednesday, and Friday, and sell their goods at a street market. We could buy everything we needed. Small boutiques would sell sugar, ice, etc.

Our home in Gros Mornes was one story, painted light green, with three rooms, a porch in front and a yard in the back. The roof was tin. We lived on Rue du Centre (Center Street) and behind us was Rue Palais (Palace Street), and in front of us was Grand Rue (Big Road/Main Street).

At the time in Haiti, handicapped kids were regarded as their parents' punishment for having done something wrong. You were cursed. It was only slightly less terrible if something happened to you and you became handicapped after you were born. Some parents even threw away their "defective" children. No one talked about that. In most cases, though, you'd simply be left at home instead of sent to school like your normal brothers and sisters. The governments didn't care. If it weren't for my mother, I probably would have grown up continuing to help in the garden.

During this period, the only school in Haiti that accepted handicapped children was St. Vincent's in Port-au-Prince. My eye doctor, Dr. Frederique, referred us there. Sister Joan Margaret, a nun with the Episcopalian mission, had started St. Vincent's in 1954. She had three students then, and they sat under a tree. To spread the word and recruit more, she traveled around the country, walking and driving, to find other students. She was a dynamic woman who beat cancer three times and lived to be ninety-nine years old.

When I turned five, my mother decided I would start school at St. Vincent's. She took me away from my friends and siblings.

THE MIRACLE OF MUSIC

I thought this was the worst day of my life. At that time, parents didn't communicate with their children as much as now. She probably assumed that I wouldn't understand the reason why the other 4 children could stay in school in Gros Mornes while I had to go away.

Port-au-Prince is normally four or five hours from Gros Mornes. But at that time the road was so bad that it used to take us over twelve hours, especially when it rained the day before we had to travel. We left early one Sunday morning, stayed with a friend of my mother's in Carrefour that night, and on Monday morning, my mother took me to be enrolled. She filled out some paperwork and said goodbye.

Goodbye? I cried and begged her to stay. "You'll be fine," she said, but I held on to her dress for dear life. This went on until she said she had to do something and would be right back. Trusting her, I let go of her dress. But she never came back. This dramatic and negative experience would stay with me for the rest of my life, and that is why I believe it was difficult for me to trust women in future relationships. After my mother walked away, the nuns tried to take me inside but I told them no, believing my mother would be right back to take me home. After a while, they told me that she would not come back, that she'd left.

I couldn't stop crying. The nuns took me to a classroom filled with children, probably to distract me. Instead, the students made fun of me. I prayed to God to protect me from these mean children, to help me survive. I was very familiar with prayers. Not only my mother would pray with us early morning and before we go to bed, I would participate in prayer sessions during certain times of the day, particularly at 12:00 p.m., listening to Radio 4VEH.

The teacher, then Muriette Charles, dressed in the red and white uniform that all the teaching staff of the school was wearing, asked me, "What's your name?

"Romel Joseph," I said.

"Where do you come from?"

"Gros Mornes Gonaïves," I sniffled.

"What's your mother's name?" she asked.

"Madame Gilberte."

"What's your father's name?

"Gilbert Joseph."

She told me to sit closer to her. Then she whispered in my ear that she was also from Gros Mornes and, in fact, was my cousin. I didn't know her and she didn't know me. I don't know if my mother even knew her, but I wasn't going to argue. She made the students stop bothering me, I could talk to her anytime, and she assured me that everything would be fine. She eventually left the school to become an Episcopal nun: Sister Claire-Marie, but while she was at St. Vincent's, her presence was a blessing. She made sure I was okay. That lasted only one short year, and after she left the teasing got worse.

The nuns always put me on a bus home for the holidays: two weeks for Christmas, two weeks for Easter, and the long summer vacation from the middle of June through the end of September. Back with my family and friends in Gros Mornes, I learned songs and games. My sister and I would always go to Grand Rivière to do laundry. Unfortunately, this wonderful Grande Rivière has the cholera virus since November 2010 and many people who used it were contaminated and died. There the women would be singing all kinds of songs and I would just sit quietly learning them. Of all these songs, "Lovana" was my favorite and is included in my album for strings. Children don't sing these old songs anymore, and that's really too bad.

I also went to a summer theater program where the drum player taught me the basic rhythms of the songs, and let me play the drums in some of the traditional Haitian pieces. I even joined the church choir because I loved to sing – that is until everyone, especially my mother, told me to stop. "Please; stop singing with that ugly voice," she said. "You are giving me a headache."

In the summer of 1966, I got "married" to a wonderful girl named Yanique who lived near us. One afternoon, at 4:00 p.m., with my sister Gilberte, and Yanique's sister Josline, as witnesses, and my brother Harry being the priest, Yanique and I were married. For a long time, we lived in a child-like way as husband and wife. She brought food for me from her house every day and we spent lots of time together, until we realized that we were being silly and the relationship faded away.

Unfortunately, my mother and I were never as close again as before I went to St. Vincent's. We didn't speak much and as I got older she lapsed into a routine of always criticizing me for something. My mother also handed out the punishments. (My father never touched me.) If I did something bad, she would beat me. If I said it hurt she would ask where and then beat me where it hurt. I definitely didn't like that about her, and I think perhaps the feeling was mutual. I don't know if she secretly disapproved of me because of my eye problems, or my attitudes, or my nonattachment to her, but she always seemed more negative than positive.

Looking back, she was actually a great mother, especially during the six years (1969-1995)when she had to take care of the five of us by herself while my father was in the States. At the end of the day, each parent has their own strategy to raise their kids.

Obviously she did a great job, because all of her five children are successful in life.

At St. Vincent's School, away from the easy safety of home, I had to live in the real world and survive in a strange environment, with people I didn't know. For all intents and purposes, I was on my own, scared and adrift. As a result, I developed trust issues and a severe inferiority complex, as the school's other handicapped students taunted me as both ugly and stupid. Even the school caretaker told me I was dumb and would never accomplish anything.

The children were truly disagreeable and horrible. For some reason which I never understood, they all believe that I was the most stupid child in the school and they would call me "Bouki." In Haitian folklore, Bouki always does stupid things and Malice does the smart things. Though now looking back at some of the stories, Bouki was actually intelligent. He always had to find the untraditional ways to be successful.

For example, one night, Bouki wanted to steal some eggs in someone's house. So Malice told him to wait until morning after the owner of the house left for work. So in a little while, Bouki went up a tree and started singing: "Cocoriko!" several times. Then Bouki went to Malice and said, "The rooster has sung. It's time to go get the eggs."

Malice looked outside and said, "No way, Bouki. It's still night time."

So in a little while again, Bouki found some wood and lit a huge fire. Then he called Malice. "Look! The sun is out. It's time to go."

Of course Malice told him, "What are you doing, Bouki? You need to wait for the real morning."

But the teasing was the least of my problems. The men responsible for taking care of us turned our dorm into a violent prison. The level of child abuse was unbelievably horrible. For example: we all had to be sitting at the table at least one hour before the food arrived, in total silence. If a child was unfortunate enough to have a cold and cough, he would be hit with an iron-like belt each time. Coughing was a real problem because it was very easy to catch a cold at the dorm since we had to get up at 5:00 a.m. and run into the cold shower. If you peed in your bed, you would be hit with the belt twenty-five to fifty times. And so on!

The expression "saved by the bell" was true for us. There was a clock in College Bird across our dorm which would give the time every thirty minutes. It was a life saver for those who peed in their beds. If you woke up and found your bed wet, you had to wait for the clock to give you the time. If you were lucky enough and it was 12, 1, 2, or even 3:00 a.m., then you would take the sheets to the bathroom, squeeze the sheets as best as you could to get the pee out, put them on the windows where it was usually windy, and wait for them to dry, up to 4:30. Once they were dry, you had to run to the room as quietly as you can so the caretakers wouldn't hear you, make the bed, and go to sleep.

The amount of food a child could receive was based on age. The younger you were, the less food you received, using a system of different-sized plates. I was always hungry because I had so little food. Periodically, my mother would make a special trip from Gros Mornes to bring me food. I asked her to stay as long as possible so I could eat. As soon as she left, the older boys and the men responsible for us would take my food away and gulp it all down.

As I found out in time, the problem was not because the school did not have enough food to give to the students -- on the contrary, it did. Various international organizations, such as Catholic Relief Services, did bring all kinds of food to the school. What happened was that the people in charge, probably unbeknownst to Sister Joan, wouldn't give it out to the students. Eventually, when these institutions would come for periodic inspections, they would find all the food locked in storage depots--spoiled and full of worms. Naturally, after these findings, the donations stopped. No more food was given to St. Vincent's School. I did pray to God to one day give me the opportunity to have enough food to eat, and my prayer was eventually answered. We also had problems with the bad spirits. The dormitory was built where there was a cemetery. And whoever built the dorm didn't exorcise the space. Consequently, all the zombies, ghosts, and dead spirits were there, coming to our rooms, touching us at night. We would hear women walking around with high-heeled shoes, strange voices, etc.

Life was hell. But as my mother used to say, "There is no prayer without amen." I didn't stop praying, hoping somehow the day would come where I would no longer be considered stupid and get beaten up constantly. Even at that early age, I learned to never give up, to always pray, and hope for the best to come.

2

Discovering the violin, (1970-1977.) prodigy, pride, a new life, travels to America, living between two worlds, the street life, love, sex.

The first part of my life, that is from birth to age five, was fun and enjoyable. The second part, that is from age five to ten, was miserable and hellish. As mentioned in the preceeding chapter, I prayed a lot. One of the prayers I would recite was, "Dear little Jesus, you said, 'Let the children come to me, for the kingdom of God belongs to them.' I am coming to you so that you may save me from this abject misery."

I especially used to get beaten up because I didn't know my lessons in class. During that time in Haiti, and still in many schools today, the student had to memorize every word in the lesson and recite it from memory. If you forgot one word while reciting the lesson, it meant you didn't study and might be punished by getting beaten up.

This was a real problem, for I was being punished every day. As I would find out later, I don't really have a great capacity for learning words by memory. Then I found a solution: use music to memorize the words.

One day, when I was eight years of age, a woman came and took me out of class. I asked her, "What have I done wrong this time?"

She replied, "I am going to teach you how to play the piano." So I went with her and she taught me one song which I still remember today. I performed the whole song at the end of the thirty-minute lesson. Then she asked me to wait. She quickly went downstairs and came back to the music room with Sister Joan.

The teacher, whose name was Gladis, asked me to play the song again. I played it once more, and Sister Joan said, "Mes compliments."

I said, "Thank you," and she left. From that moment on, I started to go into the music room frequently, listening to the older boys, such as Onickel and Ulric -- also known as Ti Pierre -- playing the piano, so I could learn from them.

One afternoon, as I was messing around on the piano, a group of girls were studying near the music room. I stopped playing and stayed quietly listening to them, and I made the great discovery. In order for Haitian students to memorize their lessons, they used three musical notes: "mi sol la." For the sake of explanation, we will use the key of "A minor natural scale."

The most common way to sing the words of the lesson is: "Mi la la sol la sol la_____, sol la la sol la mi la_____. Mi la sol la_____,mi la sol la_____,mi la sol la sol la sol la mi la_____; ending on the tonic. (The line with dashes means that the note is long.) Sometimes, the student might end the phrase on the note G, which made the phrase somewhat deceptive. For example: "Mi la la sol la sol la_____, sol la la sol la sol sol_____." Etc. A student can memorize pages and pages of a lessons rapidly by singing this musical format. Based on the fact that Haiti is a Catholic nation, this format of studying probably comes from the way the Catholic priests pray for hours using a few musical notes.

I used to study just like them, singing the words. But what I started doing differently was to not just sing the words, but doing it in a methodical musical fashion. I would assign a note to a particular phrase, as well as changing the length of certain sounds.

Example: "The United States is in North America could be: "Mi mi mi mi mi_____, mi mi mi mi mi mi la_____." Mi to la is a perfect ascending fourth.

Technically for each sentence, you create a different song with these three notes. You connect them and they constitute a long song. In this way, as long as I remembered the song, I would remember the word-phrase associated with each musical sentence, and it worked. I got hit less and less for class recitation by my teacher, and my grades improved considerably. Even more fun, after learning the lesson, I could play it on the piano while reciting for verification before going to class -- "Awesome!"

Music was already making a positive difference in my life. I became good friends with Ti Pierre, and particularly Onickel, who were both older than me, and were already good musicians. Onickel taught me how to play the drumset and the Haitian drums (Tambou), as well as handbells.

But the turning point was one morning, in May 1970. I walked in the music room, and Onickel was playing "Haiti Chéri," translated as "Haiti, darling," which was and is still one of my very favorite Haitian songs. He was playing a musical instrument that I had never seen or heard before. I stood for a while and listened. The sound was beautiful.

Once he was done playing the song, I asked him, "What is this music box?"

He replied, "It's called a violin."

"How can I learn to play that?" I asked.

Onickel said, "I can take you to Sister Joan and you can tell her that you would like to play the violin."

"Okay, I will ask her," I said. A few days later, Onickel went with me to Sister Joan.

She asked me,"What do you need?"

"I would like to learn how to play the violin," I said.

Sister Joan said,"Okay. There is a teacher who is coming from the States to teach the violin for the summer. You can work with her."

"Okay. Thank you Chère Soeur," I said. I left her office all excited, knowing soon I would start taking violin lessons.

On June 6th, at 5 p.m., the teacher was in the music room. Her name was Nina Ralph. Nina was a volunteer who came from Louisville, Kentucky. She used to teach violin in the public schools. Sister Joan assembled a group of us and Nina gave us our first lesson.

That day I made a peccadillo. Everyone was holding their violins with the left hand and the bow with the right hand. But I reversed it. All the students were making fun of me, telling me how stupid I was for holding the violin with the right hand. I was kind of ashamed, but was far from giving up. I was there to learn how to play "Haiti Chéri." Nina gently changed the violin for me, from right to left hand. My insatiable determination to master the instrument through relentless practice revealed my prodigious talent.

Within a month, I was selected to play a solo: "Song of May," from Suzuki Book One, and everyone in the concert hall was impressed. I played really well and I was happy. Then I went on vacation to Gros Mornes to be with my family, telling them about the violin.

When I came back to school in October 1970, Nina was gone. So Onickel became my teacher. By then, not only I could play "Haiti Chéri," I also learned all the Christmas songs I used to hear on the radio, as well as the religious songs; my favorite one being "Read the Bible, pray every day, and you will grow."

In January 1971, my mother came to Port-au-Prince, bringing me to school from Christmas vacation. I wanted her to hear something that no one from Gros Mornes knew. So I asked Sister Joan to allow my mother to listen to me play the violin, to which she agreed. I took my mother upstairs into the music room. Sister Joan also came along with us.

I performed three songs for her: "Away in a Manger," "I am dreaming of a White Christmas," and "Silent Night." She was impressed and cried. Unlike my singing, she said, "You will become great playing that instrument one day." Just like me in May 1970, she had never seen or heard a violin before. I guess she could discriminate between what was bad -- which was my singing -- and what was good, which was my violin playing.

That same year in August, my mother decided to leave Gros Mornes and moved to Port-au-Prince with the entire family. My father had already left for the States in 1969. She found a house in Carrefour which she shared with another woman. Now I didn't have to go to Gros Mornes anymore.

The house was surrounded by four Voodoo priests who would frequently have nightly ceremonies. I didn't mind it too much; I felt like I was in music school, learning all these traditional Haitian rhythms and songs. What did surprise me is that their Voodoo services always began with the Catholic mass. I guess they had to ask God's permission first in order to invoke the devil.

From time to time I would go visit these Voodoo priests. They liked me and they would tell me and other people who were around stories about the different spirits, their cultural and social life, where they live, which were facinating. They knew how much I loved girls, and they would always warn me to be careful picking up girls on the streets.

The fact is when you see a beautiful girl on the streets, you need to think twice about going with her to her home or put her in your car. She might be a zombie. This situation is more true today than ever because of so many people who died in Port-au-Prince during the earthquake -- there are all these zombies walking around everywhere. In fact, while I was in Port-au-Prince after my wife Myslie's funeral, I was told by many people to be very careful not to date her sister Josette, because Myslie could transform herself,by becoming her sister, to be with me. Having sex with a dead person is usually fatal. It's hard to believe that dead people have such power. But apparently in Haiti they do.

Nina came back in February 1971, and I continued working with her. My playing was improving constantly. I could play better than all the students who started with me and were making fun of me. Finally, I felt that there was something I could do that they couldn't.

I also learned all the "chansonettes françaises," which were popular French songs that everyone knew, and all the girls would want me playing for them. Cool! I had more girls for friends than I could ever imagine. I began to notice that my relationship with the violin had changed me from a once-helpless boy into a self-confident (and sometimes insufferable) young man. The attention I now received from the students and teachers – and even my mother -- evolved from ridicule to respect. My caretakers would comment, "He is ugly and stupid but plays the violin well." I was becoming more and more popular. I could play the violin, piano, drums, Haitian drums, viola, and I was a member of the handbell choir. Thus, my self-esteem was growing.

One morning, in April 1971, as I was listening to the radio, the music that was playing was abruptly stopped and I heard the announcement: "The President of Haiti, François Duvalier, is dead and will be replaced by his young nineteen-year-old son, Jean Claude Duvalier."

I remember saying, "Nineteen years old? I am twelve. I can almost be president." I was kind of scared but I didn't know exactly why.

Then on the following Saturday, there was a huge wind and all the people who were outside were running to their houses. I asked what was going on -- everyone said it was François Duvalier's funeral. And just like Jesus, his power was being felt around the country, and his son Jean-Claude Duvalier assumed the presidency.

Jean Claude Duvalier was born in Port-au-Prince on July 3rd, 1951, and was the thirty-third president of Haiti. He went into office on April 21, 1971, and was taken away from Haiti on February 7th, 1986, along with his wife Michèle Bennet, whom he married in 1980, and divorced in 1993.

He attended the most prestigious Haitian schools, College Bird and St.-Louis de Gonzague. Later, under the direction of several prominent professors, including Maitre Gerard Gourgue, at the University of Haiti, he studied law.

Jean Claude, as we called him, had little interest in government. He was a young man, wanting to have some fun, especially since he had been raised in an isolated environment. Now it was time for him to go out and make up lost time with the girls.

He was invested with near-absolute power by the constitution. He took some steps to reform the regime, by releasing some political prisoners and easing censorship on the press. However, there were no substantial changes to the regime's basic character. Opposition was not tolerated, and the legislature remained a rubber stamp.

Much of the Duvaliers' wealth came from the Régie du Tabac (Tobacco Administration). Duvalier used this "nonfiscal account," established decades earlier, as a tobacco monopoly, but he later expanded it to include the proceeds from other government enterprises and used it as a slush fund for which no balance sheets were ever kept. By neglecting his role in government, Duvalier squandered considerable domestic and foreign goodwill and facilitated the dominance of Haitian affairs by a clique of hardline Duvalierist cronies, the so-called "dinosaurs." Foreign officials and observers also seemed more tolerant toward "Baby Doc" in areas such as human-rights monitoring, and foreign countries were more generous to him with economic assistance. The United States restored its aid program for Haiti in 1971.

The interesting fact is that despite the incredibly high level of corruption and crime perpetrated by those in power during the years of President Jean Claude, 1971 through 1986 were the most peaceful years in Haiti during my lifetime. Anyone, as long as you were not known as an undesirable political person, could be on the streets twenty-four hours a day without having to worry about anything. The word "insecurity" didn't exist. The streets were clean, there were tourists everywhere, and the hotels were doing well. We had beautiful Christmas decorations on the streets; there were many movie theaters, concerts, and popular music, especially compas direct groups which flourished. The dollar was one to one -- that is, one US dollar was one Haitian dollar.

But under the surface the economic situation was deteriorating; too much money was being taken away to be sent to the US and Swiss banks. By 1979, the economic system started to really break down. Thousands of Haitians were leaving Haiti for Miami.

On May 27th,1980, Jean-Claude made a huge political and social mistake by marrying Michèle Bennett Pasquet, a mulatto divorcée with an unsavory reputation. Her first husband, Alix Pasquet, was the son of a well-known mulatto officer who had led an attempt to overthrow Papa Doc Duvalier. Although Jean-Claude himself was light-skinned, his father's legacy of support for the black middle class and antipathy toward the mulatto elite had enhanced the appeal of Duvalierism among the black majority of the population. With his marriage, Jean-Claude appeared to be abandoning the informal bond that his father had labored to establish.

The extravagance of the couple's wedding, which cost an estimated $3 million, further alienated the people. Discontent among the business community and elite intensified in response to increased corruption among the Duvaliers and the Bennetts, as well as the repulsive nature of the Bennetts' dealings, which included selling Haitian cadavers to foreign medical schools and trafficking in narcotics. Increased political repression added to the volatility of the situation.

The marriage also estranged the old-line Duvalierists in the government from the younger technocrats whom Jean-Claude had appointed, including Jean-Marie Chanoine, Fritz Merceron, Frantz-Robert Monde, and Theo Achille. The Duvalierists' spiritual leader, Jean-Claude's mother, Simone Ovide Duvalier, was eventually expelled from Haiti, reportedly at the request of Michèle Duvalier. With his wife, Duvalier had two children, François Nicolas and Anya.

As much as Michèle was disliked, and perhaps was horrible in so many ways, she was a highly prolific woman in terms of arts and culture, and because of that, I had a special love for her in my heart. She improved the quality of the main Haitian museum, "The Pantheon." She started the Ecole National des Arts (National School for the Arts). She constructed Théâtre National (National Theater), and was constantly bringing well-known artists to Haiti. I think Michèle would have created the first Haiti Performing Arts Center, which was always one of my most important dreams, had she stayed longer in power. I did cry secretly when she left while studying at the Juilliard School in 1986, wondering if my dream would ever come true. But the situation continued to worsen, and eventually Jean Claude and his family had to leave.

In response to an outbreak of African swine fever virus on the island in 1978, US agricultural authorities insisted upon total eradication of Haiti's pig population. The Program for the Eradication of Porcine Swine Fever and for the Development of Pig Raising (PEPPADEP) caused widespread hardship among the peasant population, who bred pigs as an investment. My brother, Harry, worked in that program in l'Artibonite, the part of Haiti where Gros Mornes, my birth village, is found.

It was heartbreaking to see all these pigs go, especially because of griot, one of the most popular foods and my absolute favorite. I felt that just because some pigs are sick, the fact that they all had to die was inhuman. In fact, is it conceivable if, in a town of 100,000 inhabitants, 10,000 of them have a contagious illness, then everyone in the town must be killed?

Additionally, reports that AIDS was becoming a major problem in Haiti caused tourism to dramatically decline. By the mid-1980s, most Haitians felt hopeless, as economic conditions worsened and hunger and malnutrition spread. This was the time when the middle class which François Duvalier had created really started to exit Haiti by thousands, going primarily to United States and Canada, because there was no future for them.

Moreover, widespread discontent began in March 1983, when Pope John Paul II visited Haiti. The pontiff declared, "Something must change here." He went on to call for a more equitable distribution of income, a more egalitarian social structure, more concern among the elite for the well-being of the masses, and increased popular participation in public life. Upon the departure of the Pope, Jean-Claude's government did make one change, which was "the time." They have changed the time (observance of Daylight Savings Time) every six months.

In February 1972, a new violin teacher, John Jost, came to work with us. He still comes to Haiti to this day. I studied with him from February 1972 through August 1977. He was an excellent teacher. I started to study the violin works from the standard classical repertoire with him. In October of that same year, John signed me up with the Holy Trinity Philharmonic Youth Orchestra. It was quite a new orchestra created by another Episcopal nun, Sister Ann Marie.

But I had a problem -- I couldn't read music. So John came

up with the idea to record the violin parts on tape and he would teach me the bowings once I knew the notes. I didn't use the tapes much because I had an excellent memory and perfect pitch. I learned the pieces by heart in rehearsals as well as the bowings by watching the concertmaster's bow arm. I could memorize any symphony within a few hours. Everyone was impressed. I was the new talent, the new kid on the block!

The violin was the answer to my prayer. I became more self-confident in other activities, as well as my social interactions with others. On the other hand, I also became mean and terrible toward the teachers who used to beat me, as well as my caretakers. I was becoming a VIP for both St. Vincent and Holy Trinity schools. I started to get away with bad behavior.

I had an opportunity for my favorite bad behavior every morning. Before class started, we had to sing the Haitian National Anthem, followed by prayers, and a Christian song. I would sing loud and out of tune. The teacher would be angry with me and pull my ears. I didn't like that. I felt my ears were too important and musically precious for these teachers to be messing with them. So, one morning, I put a tremandous amount of baby oil on my ears. And when they tried to pull my ears, their hands were full of oil. They were so angry, and their anger was my fun. The orchestra had its first Christmas party on December 26th. For a Christmas gift, I received an LP33 album of the life and music of Tchaikovsky. These albums were donated to the orchestra by Mr. Raul Denis, Sr., who was the owner of the only classical music store in Port-au-Prince -- "La Boîte à Musique" (translated as "The Music Box"). It was the very first Christmas gift that I had received in my life.

As soon as I got home, I listened to it and I instantly fell in love with Tchaikovsky's life and music. This album inspired me in two ways. One day, I would create my own symphony orchestra which would perform all Tchaikovsky's romantic works. But my short-term goal was to perform the Tchaikovsky concerto with the Holy Trinity Orchestra. From now on, playing "Haiti Chéri" was not an issue; my new focus was to perform the Tchaikovsky violin concerto, which is considered to be one of the most difficult works in the violin repertoire.

When I shared my exciting plan with a school administrator, he grumbled, "Why don't you pray so that we have enough food to eat!" I replied, "But Jesus said nothing is impossible if you have faith." He ignored me and walked away.

Later that evening, around 11:00 p.m., I saw a group of my older friends, six of them, going out.

"Where are you going?" I asked.

One of them answered, "Where do you think we are going at this time of night? To the prostitutes."

"To the prostitutes?" I asked.

Again he replied, "Yes, but you are too young to go. You have no experience and you will lose your money. If you want to start learning, however, then you are welcome to go with us."

I joined them and off we went to the prostitutes. I was nervous and excited. It was a new adventure. I'd never had sex with a woman before. Then we arrived on Rue du Centre (Center Street) in front of the National Prison. There was a very long line which was on both Rue du Centre and Grand Rue (Main Street). At least 300 people were in line. Center Street and Main Street run north and south. The corridors where the women have their rooms run east and west.

Each woman was in a room. The lines had people from all

walks of life – rich, poor, black, white, mulattoes, military men, Tonton Macoutes, and many great musicians. It was the social milieu to be in, in order to meet important people. In Haiti, prostitution is legal, though the women don't pay taxes. The lines moved rather quickly and finally it was my turn.

A woman in one of the rooms opened a door and said, "Who is next?"

In a scared tone of voice, I said, "Me."

She invited me to come in. I walked in and she closed the door. The room was small and smelled strange and was lit with a little gas lamp. There was only one bucket of water where everyone cleaned up. Then she said,

"You have to give me two gourdes for the moment I will spend with you." This was about twenty cents in US currency. I gave her the money and she said, "Let's go for it." I was getting even more nervous because I didn't know what to do. She said, "What's wrong with you? I don't have much time. Don't you see the number of people who are still out there?"

I told her, "It's my first time and I don't know what I am supposed to be doing."

She replied, "Take your clothes off and I will show you. Your time is running out."

I took my clothes off and she started to show me. But I was so nervous that I couldn't even get an erection. She became really frustrated and said,"This is not the place for me to teach you what to do. You need to find a teacher; then you can come back again."

I put my clothes on and left. Once I was outside of her room, one of my friends asked me, "How was it?"

I replied, "Oh, it was great! I really enjoyed myself. What a wonderful experience!" I went home, thought about what had happened, and decided to take the woman's advice by looking for a teacher.

The next evening, I went out around 7:00 p.m. by myself on Main Street, but in a different area where there were many girls and no lines. I found a really beautiful girl. Her name was Linda. We started a conversation.

I said timidly, "Hi."

Linda said, "Good evening. What would you like?"

I said, "I am looking for a woman who will teach me how to have sex."

Linda said, "Sure. I will teach you. But you have to give me enough money to stay with you for a while."

I asked, "How much?"

She said, "$2."

I figured this was like paying for school. I agreed to her price and we went to her room. I was under no pressure. She gave me a wonderful lesson on how to have sex. In all, she gave me a total of eight lessons during a two-week period. Linda was not just beautiful, but she was patient, smart, and caring. Once I completed my course, I said "goodbye" and never saw her again. I was now ready to face the long lines and the professional women, and I did great!

It was 1973 and as the new year progressed, I started to play the violin in different hotels with Ti Pierre, who accompanied me on the piano. The remuneration wasn't much. But it did help me with some basic expenses; especially food to eat. In addition, I was able to meet all kinds of people and make new friends. Moreover, I was learning some of the most popular songs from movies, and songs from other countries through the requests of various customers. Once they asked me for a song that I didn't know, I learned it for future requests.

However, one day in March 1973, one of our caretakers called a group of us together who were in the Holy Trinity Orchestra and the handbells choir, requesting that we go to the dining room. We were not sure what was going on. When we arrived, the tables were set with nice plates, spoons, knives, and forks. For my entire life, as was the case for many Haitians, I had eaten only with spoons. Then we were told that the orchestra and the bells were going to the States, and we had to learn some table manners. "To the States?" I said. "Wow!" These etiquette lessons went on for a few days, and in May, we went to the States. I didn't sleep the night before the trip. Everyone in the boys' dormitory who was travelling was celebrating. I smoked my first cigarette. For the first time in my life, I got totally drunk. I woke up with a violent headache. But I was excited. We flew from Haiti to New York's Kennedy Airport. From there, we took a bus and went to Duxbury, Massachusetts.

We performed in many cities in the United States. All in all, we did twenty-five concerts in twenty-six days. The trip was exhausting. Our last concert was in New York, at St. John's Cathedral. My father, who was living in New Jersey at the time, came to visit me. He gave me $50 to take to Haiti and share with my brothers and sister. Sadly, someone in the orchestra stole the money while I was asleep.

The next day, we flew back to Haiti. My sister Gilberte came to pick me up at Holy Trinity and took me home. During the tour, Sister Anne Marie met Mr. Wiliam Moyer, who was then Personnel Manager of the Boston Symphony. They started an exchange program between Holy Trinity and the BSO, where the orchestra members would come to Haiti not only to perform but also to work with us.

In 1974, St. Vincent's School had its own fundraising tour which featured only the handbells choir. We traveled in several towns in the US and in Canada. This trip was mainly sponsored by Compassion of Canada. During that year, I had made the decision to work more arduously in order to master the major works of the violin repertoire. I performed the Bach Concerto in A minor with the orchestra; then in 1975, the Mozart Concerto No. 4, and in 1977, the Mendelsohn Violin Concerto.

The Boston Symphony Orchestra invited the Holy Trinity Philharmonic Orchestra to Tanglewood in the summer of 1976. We were all excited. Looking now at the Boston Symphony

Orchestra membership privileges, I realize that we were really fortunate. We had private lessons, master classes, chamber music coaching, and had complete access to all rehearsals and concerts, as well as to all members of the BSO and the seductions of American culture. That was totally awesome. My teacher, Roger Chermont, was most inspiring. We had endless questions, and they had the answers.

We had the opportunity to work with fantastic musicians like Joseph Silverstein, Arthur Fiedler, Seiji Ozawa, and others -- and of course, how can I forget Tanglewood on Parade, where they performed Tchaikovsky's 1812 Overture with the participation of three orchestras, namely: (BUTI) Boston University Tanglewood Institute, (BMC) the Birkshire Music Center, and the Boston Symphony Orchestra, with real cannons, fireworks, etc. Following the Tanglewood experience, the orchestra did a tour for fundraising purposes and returned to Haiti.

During this period, the handbell choir frequently performed in churches. In one of these performances in April 1976, I met one of the most beautiful girls ever. Her name was Igénie. To me, she was as gorgeous as they come. I instantly fell in love with her. Her house was on the same street as mine. Every afternoon, before I went home, I would first go to her house and spent time with her. She loved to sing, and Radio Haiti had a Chansonnette Française ("little French songs") hour from Monday to Friday, 2:00 p.m. to 3:00 p.m. She had a notebook with all the words of the songs, and she would sing along with the radio. It was as if her voice was more beautiful than all the French women who were singing on the radio. Of course, that was a purely emotional judgment; not an objective musical one.

For a year, we were only friends. Though I was already in

love with her, I was afraid that she wouldn't recipricate my love. But on May 1st, 1977, I gathered all my courage, and wrote her a letter, asking her to become my girlfriend. She told me that she would have an answer for me by the end of the month. I waited patiently, wondering why it should take so long. But I told myself, as it is written, "Good things come to those who wait." Finally, on May 29th, she told me that she had an answer for me and she wanted to meet me at what we called "the foyer." That was at my dormitory, which was situated across from the back of the principal penitentiary of Port-au-Prince.

Many of the guards who worked for the prison were my friends. When we came home in the early morning, around 3 or 4:00 a.m. from the nightclubs, the principal doors of the foyer were locked. So we had to jump on top of the gate to get in. We had to first alert the guards, so they wouldn't think we were thieves coming to break into the school dormitory and kill us.

On June 1st, 1977, Igenie came to meet me at the school dormitory and gave me the news that she was not interested in having a relationship with me. I was crushed. I was really hoping that she would have said "yes." However, she gave me the story of a king who went to war six times and lost. Then as the king, discouraged, went sitting under a tree, he saw a spider trying to go up the tree, and each time the spider was close to the top, the spider would fall down. Finally on the seventh try, the spider made it. So the king gathered all his men, went back to war, and won. To me, that meant that if I persisted, eventually I might be successful. Of course, now I realised that I should have listened to my inner voice as opposed to her story. I should have understood the God was trying to tell me that she was not the woman for me.

Igénie and I continued to be friends; however, I shifted my focus from love to the violin -- by spending over eight hours daily practicing -- learning the Mendelssohn and the Bruch Concertos. I knew that I could always count on my violin when I was in distress.

One evening during that busy summer, a friend of mine, Michelet, came to see me. He told me that he had a friend who was getting married. He asked me if I was interested in attending the reception. I was so hungry anyway, I told him, "Sure, let's go." When we got there, everyone -- including the married couple -- was already there. They spent a few minutes giving speeches. The food smelled so good!

Then someone made the mistake of saying, "Everyone can serve themselves." Everyone flew to the table. It sounded like the January 12th earthquake. I ran toward the table; I saw someone take a whole cake. Another person took a large plate of rice. Fortunately for me, I was in front of a big turkey! So I took the plate with the turkey; I found a chair not too far from the table and ate the whole turkey. My friend took three bottles of rum and put them in the pocket of his vest, but they were taken away from him by the people who were organizing the wedding. They couldn't ask me for the turkey, because I followed one of Sister Joan's social rules which states that when you go to a social event, you can eat all you want, but never take anything with you to go home! I learned the next day that the turkey had been ordered from the States for the occasion. Oops!

Still this same summer, as I was practicing one evening, Sister Joan came to the music room with a group of visitors from Cincinnati, Ohio. She asked me to play for them, which I did. One of the visitors, Ernest Bein, was so impressed with my performance that he made the arangements for me to audition at the Conservatory of Cincinnati, Ohio in November 1977.

THE MIRACLE OF MUSIC

Once I was informed of my audition date at Cincinnati, I diverted all my attention to practicing; over 12 hours every day. I selected to perform the Bruch violin concerto for the audition.

The fateful audition day had arrived on November 6th 1978. I was first taken to a luncheon, where I performed part of the first movement of the concerto, then, my next stop was the Cincinnati Conservatory of Music (CCM) From the first floor, I took the Elevator to the third floor, and as I walked toward the audition room, I saw a beautiful young woman passing by. At once I walked to her and said with my limited English:

"What's your name?"

"My name is Mimi," she replied.

"It's nice to meet you." I said.

"It's nice to meet you, too." said Mimi.

Then I show her the piano transcription of the Bruch concerto and asked:

"This is the piece that I am going to play for my audition; is this ok?" I wanted reassurance.

"Yes," replied Mimi. "It's fine for audition."

What I didn't know is that Mimi would become my guardian angel for my first two years in college. She would work with me every week, help me preparing my violin lessons, record etudes and the different pieces that I had to learn, and help me understand some of the basic social and cultural interactions while living in the United States.

My audition went really well and I received a full scholarship to begin my studies in January 1978. I was elated because I was going to be able to study in one of the best conservatories in the United States.

I spent the months of November and December getting ready to travel to Cincinnati. During that period, I spent as much time as I could with Igenie, knowing that I probably would never see her again. But to my great surprise, on December 28th, the day before my departure, she agreed to become my girlfriend. I was happy about her decision, but sad because she made it so late. Now, while I was in school, I had to worry about a relationship which hadn't really started yet. But I loved her so much that I didn't mind. I left Haiti on December 29th, all excited about starting my musical studies, and simultaneously crying because I was leaving Igénie behind. It was a truly bittersweet feeling.

3

(1978-1983) Cincinnati Conservatory, learning English, racism, the real music world.

It's amazing how sometimes you are being prepared for your life's mission even as a child, without knowing of such preparation. Though I had a wonderful childhood from birth to five years old, (1959-1964,) the next six years -- that is from five to eleven years old (1964-1970) -- were simply miserable, and I was helpless and hopeless.

At ten years of age, my prayer was answered. I was introduced to the violin, which became the true love of my life. Though I had decided to master it, I knew little about concervatories or universities. But God in his plan created the possibility for me to continue the road toward the mission he had for me. I was going to go to Cincinnati Conservatory of Music (CCM).

I was excited because I was among the first students of the orchestra to travel to the States for higher studies. I knew that I had the talent; I was ready to work hard and I would be successful. My self-confidence was extremely high. However, in the previous trips, I had been under the protection of the sisters and around all my friends. This time, I would be all alone, in a world that I didn't know. In addition, not only I was blind, I spoke very limited English. These factors created a feeling of nervousness within me. But I knew that I was going to be all right, for it was God's plan.

On December 29th, 1977, I said goodbye to all my friends, to my family, and Igenie, and flew with a group of missionaries in a small private plane to Lynchburg, Virginia. I arrived there around 11:00 p.m. We deplaned and had to walk outside for about two minutes to the building. I wasn't dressed properly for the nasty cold that was outside. It felt as if I were being stabbed by sharp knives and I was in terrible pain. I could no longer feel my fingers. I started crying, saying, "I am going to die." The missionaries walked quickly with me to the building. I felt as if I had been outside for hours.

Finally I was in the warm building, but I still had no feeling in my fingers. So they made me put my fingers under very warm water. Oh my God! I started screaming. The pain was excrutiating. Apparently, the water was too hot for my fingers. It took over two weeks for any feeling to return back to my fingers, and I couldn't play the violin during these days.

The next day, I was flown to Cincinnati. Arrangements were made for me to stay at a YMCA-like place which was near the Conservatory. I spent the first day of school registering for classes with the help of a wonderful lady. I believe her name was Gloria Berk. They signed me up for orchestra, a music theater theory class (as opposed to the regular theory class because I came in the middle of the year); introduction to conducting which I hated because it was at 8:00 a.m. which meant I had to get up early; violin, piano, and English as a second language (ESL).

Another obstacle I faced was that I couldn't see well enough to find my classes since I couldn't read the signs or classroom numbers or even find the buildings; for most of the buildings look alike -- that is, they had the same color, and to me, approximately the same architecture. However, at the YMCA, I met Ed West, who was a pianist at CCM. We quickly became friends, and he did a day of orientation with me, showing me how to find all my classes and how to identify each building. Not only that, I went to him when I had problems understanding the lessons, especially music theory, and he made sure that I understood everything. He was a Godsend.

I loved most of my classes, particularly my theory class. I was the star of the class, as the only one with perfect pitch. As a new student, all the other students assumed that I wouldn't be able to do ear training. But to their and the teacher's great surprise, I knew all the chords or notes that were being played. When there was a test, the students would try to sit next to me so I could tell them the name of the notes or chords. Since I didn't know the names of the notes or chords in English, my teacher, Chris Anderson, worked with me after class, giving me the English equivalents for the notes and chords.

I was assigned to the first violin section of the Concert Orchestra. It was strange, because I was the only black orchestra member -- everyone was white. Coming from Haiti, that was unfamiliar to me. But I didn't mind; it was part of the process and at that time, I didn't really think anything about it.

For their first concert, among the pieces they were playing was *Petrushka* by Stravinsky. Though I came to love that work, I felt sick listening to it. It sounded like everyone was playing the wrong notes. In Haiti, we only listened to music up to the end of the 19th century. I memorized all the other pieces and asked the conductor to allow me not to play *Petrushka* , and he agreed. He was right; I didn't have the musical knowledge to memorize such a difficult work.

In order to play in orchestra, I had friends recording the violin parts for me. But it wasn't the same as it was in Haiti. The pieces were much longer and much more challenging. Unbeknownst to me, my first quarter at the conservatory was like a test. Everyone, including Rev. Ernest Bein who first heard me play in Haiti, as well as my violin teacher, Mr. Jens Illerman, and others wanted to see if in my condition I could study at the conservatory. I did what I was supposed to do -- that is, pray and work hard.

In the middle of January 1978, Rev. Bein came back from vacation and I moved to his house with his wife, Mary, and their two dogs "Easy" and "Chappy." Easy was a basset and his ears dragged on the floor because they were so long. Though I enjoyed being in school, I did miss my friends and family, especially Igénie with whom I had excellent correspondence and phone conversations from time to time.

These first few days were so warm that I was wondering and asking the students if Cincinnati would be cold. They told me to wait and see. By the end of the month, the snow had started and we had over twenty feet of it for that particular winter. I was totally excited, for I had never seen or experienced snow in my life. The first day it was (0) degrees Farenheit, I asked Mary to let me go outside without a shirt so I could feel what it was like to be outside in such cold weather. She agreed, I then went outside for as long as I could stay, and came back in all excited and happy. I took many pictures in the snow. But unfortunately they were lost in The Victorian School fire of January 12th, 2000.

Though I had a wonderful time in the snow, I did miss my friends and family terribly, especially Igénie. We wrote to each other practically every week, and we conversed on the phone from time to time. I would ask Mary and Rev. Bein how possible it would be to bring Igénie to the States to be with me. Of course I wouldn't have asked such a question if I were thinking; for financially it probably would have been very difficult if not impossible.

At the end of March, James Smith and Mark Bauer, my two piano teachers that I had when I was in Haiti from 1972 through 1977, organized a fundraising concert for me in Evanston, Illinois, with the participation of Gérard Dupervil, who was then one of the most popular Haitian singers, with other artists from Northwestern University. The hall was full and the concert was magnificent.

Upon my return to Cincinnati, Mary and Rev. Bein had a great surprise for me. They told me my grades had arrived and I had "A" for my classes. Mary said, "You have a 4.0. Congratulations!" I was confused because in Haiti, the grade system went from 0 -- which is the worst grade -- to 10, the best grade.

I said, "I don't understand -- what's the worst grade here?

Mary replied, "'F' is the worst grade." They realized that I didn't even understand the American grading system, and they took sometime to explain it to me. Up to December 1979, I had 4.0.

For the last quarter, that is from April to June, Rev. Bein decided to have me live at the dorm, which was Calhoon Hall. I wasn't too happy at first because again, I would be by myself. But it didn't take long for me to start enjoying life at Calhoon. I made many friends, and I went out with girls on weekends to concerts, restaurants, and the like.

I used to practice in my room in the evening after dinner, until one evening while I was practicing, I heard a knock on my door. I opened the door and four black men came in. One of them said, "What's wrong with you?"

I said, "Excuse me? I don't understand."

Another one continued, "Why are you playing this trashy white people's instrument?"

I answered, "I am from Haiti, and I didn't know that white people had their own instruments."

Another one stated, "Why don't you play the saxophone instead?

I replied, "Well, I will take your suggestion into consideration."

And they left. Since that day, I never practiced in my room again; I stayed at the conservatory practice room instead where it was safer.

That was my first true introduction to racism and I started asking my friends questions about interactions between black and white people at the university and in the city. In addition, I took a class on sociology, and I learned so much about that part of American culture; for in Haiti, I knew of economic differences between people, but not so much about color differences. Nevertheless, I had to focus on my goal no matter what, which was to learn how to play the violin well.

The most amazing thing to me at the dorm was the food. As I wrote in a previous chapter, when I told one of my caretakers that my dream was to one day have a symphony orchestra that would perform all Tchaikovsky's works, he replied, "Why don't you pray for us to have food to eat?" He was right; we had little food to eat, and I did pray God to one day give me the opportunity to have enough food to eat. My prayer was answered.

We had twenty meals per week, and on Sunday night we had to find our own meal. I couldn't understand why the students were complaining that the dorm food was bad. There was everything, including all kinds of drinks, salads, fruit, gallons of different kinds of ice cream (which I love), immeasurable amounts of peanut butter, and no limitations to how much one could eat.

It was a dream come true. I would take three trays, full of different food, and eat, and eat, and eat. Once I was done, I took the trays to some kind of escalator, and the trays would go down somewhere to be cleaned up. At first, I couldn't put the trays on the escalator properly and these trays full of dishes would fall down and all the plates would break. After a few days, they must have sent someone to see who was doing that and I was found! So a lady, taking an empty tray, showed me how to place it properly while the escalator was moving. Since then, I never had any more accidents with the trays.

In the summer of 1978, my violin teacher, Mr. Illerman, made the necessary arangements for me to go to the Aspen Summer Music Festival for ten weeks. I had the best of times. The students there came from all over the world. The weather was wonderful, though a little dry. I did an orchestra audition, and I was put in the first violin section of the Philharmonia Orchestra.

In Aspen, I also met Alberto Esposito, who became my best friend for the next four years. Though he was only fifteen, he was super-intelligent. His English was impeccable, and I learned most of what I know of the English language from him.

While in Aspen, I wanted to learn the violin with Dorothy Delay as well. But getting to her was nearly impossible. Everyone wanted to study with her, and the line to get to her was always long. I figured that maybe one day, I would find her.

The day did come when one afternoon, I went to a concert; during intermission, Ms. Delay was standing near the music hall talking to someone. This was my chance, I said to myself. So I went and stood right behind her. As she moved back, she stepped on my foot. I dropped myself on the ground, pretending to be in pain. She apologized furiously, asking me if I was okay. She took my hands and helped me get up. I felt flattered that she was holding my hand. I asked her if I could come to one of her master classes. And she said "yes." I was happy and walked away. For the rest of the Aspen Festival, I went to all of her master classes and she usually gave me a short private lesson following some of the master classes. She was a genius when it came to violin teaching.

At the end of the festival, Mark Bauer, my former piano teacher from Haiti, whom I mentioned previously, came and picked me up. He drove from Aspen to Chicago where his girl-friend was living. There we stayed for a few days, and then we went to Cincinnati to his sister's house, where I spent the rest of the summer.

My second year at CCM, just like the first year, was very pro-ductive. I continued mastering the violin and enjoying my class on history of western civilisation, because I love history and the teacher was excellent. I was having a great social life, though sometimes I ran into trouble.

In the practice room hall on the fourth floor, I saw a friend of mine passing by. She had a nice dress on. I told her, "I like to see you on a dress."

"What?" she said. "You like to see me undress?" Then she said, "OOOOOOOOOOOOOOOOH! You don't speak English yet. You mean to say you like to see me *in* a dress."

I said, "Yes, in a dress." I was having a preposition problem which made her angry at first, but she of course quickly understood the problem and everything was okay between us.

One day, I met a girl whose name was Susanne. She was white, very attractive, and played the harp. I asked her to go out and she agreed. Apparently she must have told her father who was a teacher at the university, for the next day, she came to me and said, "I am sorry. I won't be able to go out with you because my father does not want me to date black men."

I told her, "That's fine; I understand." But actually I didn't understand. I wasn't prepared to deal with racism. Alberto was instrumental in explaining to me in detail the reality of ratial discrimination in Cincinnati, which is pretty much a Southern city. I kept on telling myself that I was not from the United States; therefore, I didn't have to worry myself about the problem of racism. I just had to stay away from those who were racists, whether they were black or white people; then I would be fine.

Sometimes, I also had cultural problems. One afternoon, I saw Mimi, the first woman I met before my audition on November 1977. I said, "Wow! Mimi, congratulations! You gained lots of weight. That's nice."

Mimi said, "What! You are so mean!"

Then I realized that I had made a mistake. In Haiti at that time, telling a woman she had gained weight was a compliment, while in the States, it was not the thing to say.

I said, "I am sorry, Mimi. I made a cultural mistake."

Mimi said, "Oh, that's okay. I understand." Then she got over it.

For my second year, I was still in concert orchestra. But everyone was so busy that it was getting more difficult to find people to record the first violin part for me. Sometimes, if the piece wasn't too difficult, I would learn during orchestra rehearsals.

One afternoon, during a rehearsal, the orchestra was working on Mozart's Symphony No. 36. I was sitting next to a girl whom I didn't know. However, she was really nice. I asked her her name and she said, "Cecilia." She must have known of my situation, since we had the same violin teacher. I listened to her play and when there was a passage I didn't hear too well, she would play it for me. By the time the two hours of rehearsal were over, I had the whole symphony memorized. She had no idea how I was able to memorize so fast. We are still great friends up to this day.

This problem was resolved when I learned that the library had a closed-circuit TV for partially sighted people which enlarged the letters or musical notes up to sixty-four times bigger. I was able to use that equipment to learn all my music.

As Christmas vacation approached, I wanted to go to Haiti to see Igénie. As soon as the quarter was over in December, I flew to Haiti and Igénie and I had the most wonderful Christmas together. We went everywhere, particularly "La Caye Disko," where my best friend, Ti Pierre was on the keyboard, and Claudette, an excellent singer, would perform dancing music. I asked Igénie to please wait for me to finish my studies, then we would get married, and she agreed. I went back to the States happy, looking forward to the next time I would see Igénie, which would be next Christmas.

THE MIRACLE OF MUSIC

In March 1979, I joined the handbells choir on a tour to Canada organized by Compassion of Canada. I was once again happy to be among my friends, playing music together, and Sister Joan was very excited to have me with the group; I was a success story which would help raise even more money for the school.

The days went really fast, and in December 1979, I went back to Haiti to be with Igénie. But this time, she was very cold. She kept on saying that she didn't have time to see me because of her school. Then I learned the horrible news. She had become Ti Pierre's girlfriend. When I approached Ti Pierre, he confirmed the rumor. He told me, "Yes, you have the right information. Igénie is my girlfriend."

I asked him, "You know how much I love her -- why couldn't you have picked someone else?"

He replied, "You are in school in the States, not in Haiti, and you don't have money to take care of her. Therefore, she picked me as her boyfriend instead of you. Don't you see how she is telling you that she is busy, and yet, she is here every day with me?"

He was right. Though she told me she had lots of work for school, every day when I came to visit Ti Pierre, Igénie was always there with him. The fact is, Ti Pierre was very rich because he had been touring all over Haiti and internationally, plus he had made at least nine LP albums. In addition, his weekend performances were extraordinarily lucrative.

It was as if my life was over. I told him that I wished the two of them luck and I left. I didn't have the courage to confront Igénie about Ti Pierre's confirmation because I knew that if I were to have a second confirmation from her, I would have probably had a nervous breakdown. After all, I couldn't see any reason why Ti Pierre would lie to me.

Despite my anger at what he did, I still had great admiration for his musical talent. So the day before I was to travel back to the States, I played the violin on one of his albums, with Claudette singing. That evening, I went to Igénie's house; I spent some time with her family in Carrefour, then around 9:30 p.m., I left. She took me to the main road, which is National Route No. 2; we said a long goodbye as I felt my heart being torn to shreds, and we went our separate ways.

I spent months crying. My grades were dropping. I was no longer interested in school and I simply wanted to die. This time, it seemed even my violin wasn't going to save me. The situation was so hopeless that Alberto, who was so helpful, and some of my other friends suggested to me to seek professional help, which I did. I was lucky to see an excellent psychologist. She and I had several sessions together and she somehow got me out of my extended depression enough to go back, focusing on music and my violin.

When I went back to Haiti in 1983, I went for a last time to Igénie's house to see her again. The objective was emotional closure. My brother, Herbert, went with me. When I got there, I saw her, sitting on a small chair, with a radio near her, singing some of the popular French songs of the time. This time, I didn't know the songs because I was out of the country. I spent a few minutes at her house near her without saying a word, then I said goodbye. Once outside, I cried a little, and I told myself "Now, I can move on."

She and I didn't speak again until January 2009 when my friend Onickel called me in Haiti and told me, "Guess who is on the other line?"

I said, "I don't know."

Then Igénie heard my voice and knew who I was. It took me a while to know who she was. It was a surprise encounter. Onickel didn't tell me or Igénie that he was going to connect us together.

I was very happy to talk to her again. Though I was able to stay away from her, my love had never ended for her. We spoke frequently on the phone about the past and the present, and finally, I told her why our relationship thirty years ago had ended. She at first appeared to have no idea of what I was talking about. Then she said the whole story wasn't true. She was never Ti Pierre's girlfriend. She added it was because I didn't trust her -- that was why I didn't confront her or even believed Ti Pierre story's. Now, she said, because Ti Pierre was dead, she had no way of proving that she was right.

She might be right. But I asked her, "If Ti Pierre was wrong, how come then after my departure in 1979, you never contacted me, you never sent me a letter or called me? I could have been sick, in the hospital. If you did care, wouldn't you be concerned?" She replied that once she didn't hear from me, she assumed that I had a girlfriend in the States and had given up on our relationship. I still cannot determine who among them was really telling the truth. Nevertheless, it's too late. She is now married with two children and is going on happily with her life. But she was my first love, and I will always remember her.

I was with Ti Pierre on Wednesday afternoon, January 23rd,1991, around 4:00 p.m. at a friend's house, which was the last time we were together. That was five days before his death. Ti Pierre reconfirmed with more elaboration his past relationship with Igénie, saying, "Igénie and I dated from 1979 through 1982. Our relationship ended when I decided to take a girl named

Lolotte, who was a well-known artist in a theater group, to my first African tour in June 1982. Igénie felt humiliated and ended the relationship."

At the end of the day, I guess Igénie and I were not destined to be married. But few people ever have the opportunity to marry their first love. They just learn from the experience and move on, which is what I did.

I spent the summers of 1981 and 1982 at Tanglewood, studying the violin with Joel Smirnoff, who was then a member of the Boston Symphony Orchestra. He was a great teacher and I learned so much from him on the technical and musical aspects of the violin.

I graduated from CCM in June 1982, with a bacheler's degree in music and violin performance. then I went to Perkins school in Watertown, Massachusetts to learn piano tuning. While in the area, I continued studying the violin with Mr. Smirnoff.

At first, I was residing in Brookline and I used to go out frequently, especially on weekends. I would come home around 3 or 4:00 in the morning. I was frequently stopped by the police. They couldn't understand what a black person was doing late at night on the streets of Brookline.

So one night, around 4:00 a.m., as I was going home coming from a nightclub, walking with my white cane, a police car stopped in front of me, and a police officer said, "What are you doing outside here in this neighborhood?"

I replied, "I didn't know there was a coup d'état in the States. Is there a curfiew which I am violating?"

He said some profanities and left.

Then I moved to Roxbury to stay in a house near St. Monica's Convent, where the Episcopal sisters were and still reside. That house belonged to Rev. Reid and his wife, Sondra. They were and still are my great friends. I used to spend hours talking to Sondra about everything and anything. But at that time I used to have fun taking the bus from Roxbury to Symphony Hall, where everyone on the bus was black. Then, upon arriving at Symphony Hall, all the black people would leave the bus, and they were replaced by white people who would go all the way to Harvard Square. How facinating!

I graduated from Perkins School for the Blind in June 1983 and I moved to Haiti to spend some time working with the students at St.Vincent and St.Trinity schools. My experiences at CCM, Aspen International Music Festival, Tanglewood, and the Perkins School for the Blind will stay with me for the rest of my life. I learned a lot musically and academically. I had the opportunity to meet some wonderful individuals, and I will cherish these wonderful years.

4

(1983-1987) The wild life in Haiti, married life, Rosicrucians and mysticism, Juilliard, choice of career in music.

In June 1983, after completing my studies at the Perkins School for the Blind in piano tuning, I decided to take a recess from studying and return to Haiti for a while to share with others what I had learned in the states for the past five years. But as I have mentioned in a previous chapter, I had to first emotionally terminate permanently with Igénie, which I successfully did.

I spent the month of July in Leogane, a small town south of Haiti where Holy Trinity Orchestra has had its annual summer camp since 1971. Unfortunately, the January 12th, 2010 earthquake destroyed the whole compound. There I worked with many of the students, especially some of them who were preparing for college auditions.

While I was in Leogane, Harry, my older brother, came to see me and informed me that Jean Maret, our youngest brother, was terribly ill. We all had to find money to pay to save him. His problem was that my father, who died in December 1982, was still in the house, bringing food at night to Jean Maret and he ate the food. Now, not only Jean Maret had to be treated, but a special ceremony "exorcism" had to be done to remove my father from the house and help him find his way. Jean Maret was treated, and my father was sent away to wherever he was supposed to be. My guess is in heaven.

For the rest of the summer, together with my brother Herbert, I went everywhere in Port-au-Prince, tuning pianos. I was the only piano tuner in town, and there were many pianos that needed tuning. Besides being paid for the work, we were able to meet really interesting people wherever we went. We were considered special because we were the only choice in this profession for virtually the entire country. But one could feel the atmosphere in the country was different than it had been a few years before. Though the streets were still safe, the political, social, and economic situation was degrading.

As I have mentioned in previous chapter, in 1980, the president had married Michèle Bennett, the American-educated daughter of a well-to-do Haitian coffee merchant. At a cost of $3 million, the ceremony and festivities garnered infamy for their entry in the Guinness Book of World Records as the most expensive wedding ever held.

The same year, a son, François-Nicholas, was born. Michèle Duvalier outmaneuvered her mother-in-law in 1983 and became First Lady of Haiti. By then it had become clear that the new first lady was the power behind, next to, and perhaps in front of the throne. She began making executive decisions whenever her husband was otherwise engaged driving race cars or cruising in his presidential yacht.

THE MIRACLE OF MUSIC

In the 1984 election to Haiti's fifty-nine-seat National Assembly, no opposition candidates were permitted to contest the election. The only plausible leaders of contrary parties were specifically excluded. Gregoire Eugene, who had earlier been exiled to New York, was prevented from returning. Silvio Claude was arrested and tortured. Sixty of his followers were also arrested or exiled. So few Haitians voted that the government refused to reveal the turnout. The few meetings called to protest the elections were broken up by thugs. Duvalier confined his own electioneering to throwing money from the window of his speeding car.

In October, I became the Music Director at St. Vincent's School, teaching violin, viola, and directing the handbell choir. I also worked at Holy Trinity School with most of the string players of the orchestra. In addition to performing in concerts.

Since my departure to the States in 1978, I had not performed a recital in Haiti as of yet. So I decided to present a recital. But there was no pianist to accompany me. Consequently, Onickel told me to contact Madame Micheline Laudun Denis. He told me that she was the greatest Haitian pianist. Thus, one day in August, I called her. She wasn't to happy to talk to me, because I woke her up. Nevertheless, she told me to bring some music in the afternoon at 5:00 p.m. for what I would call an audition. At 5:00, a friend of mine, Linda Machan, went with me to Madame Denis's school, "Promusica," which was located in Turgeau. I brought her the pieces that I wanted to play for the recital. We first read Camille Saint-Saens's "Introduction and Rondo." She was so impressed that she called her husband, Mr. Raoul Denis, to come right away. When he arrived, Madame Denis and I read the Glazunov violin concerto.

We instantly became music partners. I loved her playing, and she loved mine as well. So we scheduled a recital for October 28th at the French Institute concert hall, which was designed and built by architect/engineer and violinist Fritz Benjamin. This recital was very important, for it would be the first time since 1978 that the elite classical music audience would come to hear me. I put my social life aside for a while, and focused exclusively on the recital.

It was a tremendous success. The hall was completely full. The program included: "Praeludium and Allegro" by Fritz Kreisler, Mozart Sonata No. 21 in E minor, K. 304, the Beethoven "Spring" Sonata in F Major, the Saint-Saens "Introduction and Rondo," and the Glazunov Concerto. From that night on, I was recognized as the best Haitian violinist to this day.

Following the recital, we all went to Splendid Hotel for a sumptuous reception. There was a variety of food and most of the people who attended the concert were present. I don't know how they found out about the reception because I didn't know myself. But they were present, and I was able to meet the cream of Haiti's culture.

One of my most memorable days of that period was a wonderful concert which was presented in December at the Rex Théatre by Ansy Dérose, one of the great Haitian artists of the 20th century. Ansy was a trained classical singer, guitarist, and an excellent choreographer. In addition, he was a great engineer and architect. The orchestra had all the old-time musicians that I used to dream that one day I would meet, including Raoul Guillaume, Webert Sicot, Yolande Desrose, Almando, and others.

I had the privilege of playing a violin solo, and the piece that I performed was "Noël des orphelins," translated as "Christmas for the orphans," known to me when as was a child as "Papa Noël." I was accompanied by Ti Pierre on the piano. The composer, Raoul Guillaume, was emotionally moved and the public loved the interpretation of the song, singing along as I played. They were mostly children during the time the song was written. Mr. Guillaume still talks about this performance. From then on, I performed many concerts at Holy Trinity, at the American ambassador's home, and for fundraising activities.

I spent most of my free time accomplishing one objective, which was to have lots of fun, date as many women as possible, and know all the entertainment places in Port-au-Prince. One of my favorite places, La Caye Disco, where I used to go with Igénie, was no longer a place of attraction. Claudette and Ti Pierre were having personality conflicts and the public abandoned them. I wasn't too happy about that; but oh well, life goes on.

Every Sunday, I went to a different beach, including: Ibo beach, Jolie Beach, Guylou Beach, etc. I also went to practically all the restaurants, spending many nights in different hotels, especially those I used to play in when I was younger. But now, I was a visitor with my own dates. I also went to the different movie theaters and nightclubs.

One of the girls I was dating, Betty Burford, introduced me to the teachings of the Rosicrucian Order (AMORC). She gave me a copy of the mastery of life, which I thought was fascinating. So in 1983, I became a member of AMORC, the English division in San Jose, California, until 1988. I learned many important life concepts in their teachings which I have used throughout my life in different circumstances.

In September 1984, I received a letter from Rachel Edensworth, who was in charge of the Cultural Division of the

American Enbassy, as well as the person responsible for the different grants, including the Fulbright Grant. So I went to see her, and she gave me the application. I needed someone to help me complete the paperwork, so I asked Sherry Seighman, who had been a volunteer at St. Vincent's School since 1983, to assist me. I offered to pay her, but she told me that in return, I would owe her a dinner; a condition to which I agreed.

After she was done with the forms, we turned them in, and I kept my promise by taking her out to dinner, which in effect became our first date. From then on, we continued dating, going to some of the most fun places in Port-au-Prince and its surroundings. Sherry was a highly intelligent, well-educated, creative, and multi-talented woman.

In January 1985, I received a call from Rachel, who said, "Your application was approved. You were awarded the Fulbright Grant." I was all excited. I called Sister Joan, then Sherry, giving them both the good news.

In the meantime, I filled out an application for the Manhattan School of Music and The Juilliard School. My auditions were in March for both places. First, I auditioned at the Manhattan School. All went well. Then the next morning, I auditioned at The Juilliard School.

As I was waiting in front of the audition room with other applicants, one of them, a girl, who was warming up, kept on playing extremely difficult passages of various concertos. Then she came to me and said, "Hi! Where are you from?" I assumed she was asking me that question because I was the only black person there.

I answered, "I am from Haiti."

Then she said, "You mean there is classical music there?"

I replied, "To some extent, yes." Then she walked away. I learned later it was supposed to be a strategy to psych me out.

In a few minutes, the door opened and they called her. She played some scales, and part of an etude that I'd never heard before. Then, she played the Mendelssohn Concerto. Her playing was just perfect. When she finished playing the cadenza, she stopped. But Dorothy Delay asked her to continue. Unfortunately, the girl didn't practice the part that followed the cadenza. It was like day and night. The second part sounded as if she didn't know how to play. Then, she came out crying.

I told her, "I hope you will learn your lesson and study the whole work for an audition in the future." She looked at me for one second and mumbled some nasty words and left. I am sure I received a dirty look. It's good sometimes when you are blind. You don't get to see the dirt the world is throwing at you. My teacher told me that she was rejected. I returned to Haiti, and two weeks later, I received acceptance letters from both schools, and I opted for Juilliard.

Since the Igénie experience, I decided that I would never have a long-distance relationship. So Sherry and I were engaged in April 1985, and were married legally on June 7th, 1985, and publicly on July 12th, 1985 at the Methodist Church in College Bird. Performing at this ceremony were the church choir, the handbells choir, the great Haitian soprano Nicole St. Victor, Madame Denis, and the Holy Trinity Philharmonic Orchestra.

Following the ceremony, we went to New York on July 16th. In the many life dreams that I had, being in New York was one of them. So on July 16th, we embarked for the city that doesn't sleep. We were able to find a small studio apartment right away in Clinton Hill, across from St. Joseph's College, where Sherry was hired to work in Admissions. It didn't take me long to travel from our apartment to Juilliard -- about forty minutes. I just had to take the G train, and transfer on Flatbush to the A train, then either walk to Juilliard, or take the number 1 train.

My experience at Juilliard was wonderful. I had excellent teachers for my different classes. The late Ms. Margaret Pardee, who was my principal violin teacher, was like a mother to all her students. She was a fantastic violin teacher. I still remember her every time I play the violin, because when I arrived at Juilliard, I had a horrible violin and she decided to give me another one, which I still use. I always kept it in my bathroom, and miraculously, God saved it from the notorious January 12th earthquake. It was made by Donald McKinley, and Anne McKinley, who read my story in the newspaper, decided to repair the damage.

I had lots of fun working with Ms. Liliane Fuchs, who was an inspiring violist and chamber music teacher. I didn't make many friends at Juilliard because following classes, I always went straight home. But unlike all that I had heard about Juilliard before my arrival there -- that is, how cold the people there were -- I found that it was a very friendly school and the students there were warm and sociable.

I graduated from Juilliard in May 1987. At that time, I had to make an important decision. Either I stayed in the States pursuing a career as a concert violinist, or I would go back to Haiti and work. I thought and prayed about it, and I opted to go back to Haiti. I made this life choice because I felt that first, music had done a lot for me and I should give the children of Haiti the same opportunity. After all, I had received years of musical training and had successfully completed my musical studies without spending a dime on my part. Therefore, it was logical to give back some of the knowledge that I had acquired. Secondly, part of the Fulbright requiment was that the grantee should go back and share his/her knowledge with those in his country for two years.

Thus, in June 1987, Sherry and I returned to Haiti. When we got there, It was like arriving in hell. It was a strike day; there were burning tires and soldiers of the military were shooting everywhere. It was so quiet when we left Haiti on July 1985 -- what happened that changed Haiti from what I knew to be a peaceful nation to a virtual war zone?

Upon the death of François Duvalier in 1971, with the help of his paramilitary force, the Tontons Macoutes, Jean-Claude "Baby Doc" Duvalier assumed the presidency and also declared himself president-for-life. The Duvaliers' rule was characterized by repressive state control, including the lack of basic democratic rights. Faced with economic collapse and a popular uprising, Jean-Claude Duvalier fled to France on February 7th, 1986. The period immediately after his departure was marked by mob vengeance against members of the *Tontons Macoutes*. The Haiti I knew had disappeared forever.

From 1986 to 1990, Haiti was ruled by a series of provisional governments. Weekends were always worrisome because that's when the coups d'état would take place. Night life had virtually disappeared, there were strikes almost every day, and schools could hardly function.

In March 1987, a constitution was ratified that provided for an elected, bicameral parliament; an elected president who served as head of state; and a prime minister, cabinet, ministers, and supreme court appointed by the president with the parliament's consent. The Haitian constitution also provided for political decentralization through the election of mayors and administrative bodies responsible for local governments.

On November 29ᵗʰ, 1987, the first democratic election was met with tremendous violence. From January 1988 through February 1991, Haiti went through numerous governments. And finally, in December 1990, the level of hope for a better future for all Haitian citizens in the country and abroad was high. For the first time in Haiti's history, a Catholic priest was going to be president. Jean-Bertrand Aristide won 67% of the vote in a presidential election that international observers deemed largely free and fair. Aristide took office on February 7th, 1991, but was overthrown on September 30ᵗʰ of that same year in a violent, well-orchestrated coup led by army elements and supported by many of the country's economic elite.

Going back to our return to Haiti in June 1987, this situation was unfamiliar to both of us, especially to Sherry who was seven months pregnant with our daughter, Victoria. Such political instability never existed under Duvalier father or son. We spent the night at Lesly and Yves-Rose Philippe Auguste's home; Yves-Rose was also a member of Holy Trinity Philharmonic Orchestra. They resided close to the airport and the roads were too dangerous for us to go to St. Vincent's School, which was located one block from the National Palace in the heart of Port-au-Prince. The next day, things died down somewhat, and we were able to get to St. Vincent's School, where we resided for one year.

On August 12ᵗʰ, around 1:30 p.m., as I was playing dominos in the foyer of my old dormitory with my friends, Sherry came in, saying,"It's time."

"It's time for what?" I asked.

"It's time to have the baby; the contractions have begun."

"Are you sure?" I asked.

Sherry said, "Yes, my water broke."

"How frequent are the contractions?" I asked.

Sherry said, "Every ten minutes."

I said, "Let's wait for the next contraction to be sure."

Sherry said, "Okay."

I kept on playing dominos; then in a few minutes, she had another contraction. I guessed it was for real. We called her doctor, and then we went to St. Vincent's, where Sister Joan sent us to the hospital. Once we got there, the nurses prepared her for labor. But there was a problem. They didn't have the serum to set up an IV drip, and it was a strike day. Most of the pharmacies were closed. So Sister Joan sent out looking everywhere for the serum.

By the time they found it around 6:30, Victoria had already been born at 6:12 p.m. We were all excited. She was a beautiful six-pound, twelve-ounce girl. Then I went home, giving everyone the news. Victoria came home on August 14th. We were surrounded by visitors who wanted to see the baby. Sister Joan, who at that time was having tremendous difficulty with her feet, walked all the way up to the second floor of the building to personally bring flowers to Victoria. We had purchased most of what we needed to take care of Victoria in the States. So those frequent strike days were not so bothersome.

I continued my work as Music Director for St. Vincent's School, teaching violin at Holy Trinity, and I was also employed at the new "Ecole Nationale des Arts." Socially and culturally, Port-au-Prince wasn't as fun as it used to be. The concept of insecurity, which started after the departure of Jean-Claude Duvalier, had become part of everyday life. People could no longer stay out at night without the great risk of being killed. There were strikes almost every day about something; schools could hardly function, it was a pure mess.

Sherry continued her work as volunteer at St. Vincent's School as Sister Joan's personal assistant. In addition, she was employed at the Haitian American Institute as an English instructor, as well as at Holy Trinity as the string and piano repair technician. In the summer of 1986, Sherry had learned basic stringed instrument repair with Joe Tripodi, a violin maker, while we were in New York, and in May 1987, she learned basic piano repair at the Perkins School for the Blind. With both of us working full time and a new baby to take care of, this was the continuation of a new, happy life.

5

(1987-1999) Returning to Haiti, teaching, struggling to start my academic and music school, marriage complications, the Miami experience.

In June 1987, Sherry and I returned together from New York to Haiti, a country torn with political and economic turmoil. We were living in a small room at St. Vincent's School, busy taking care of Victoria and our work in the different institutions. I continued to perform many concerts around Port-au-Prince and in Cap Haitian, just as in 2003. I was particularly interested in developing an instructional method for strings. So I have started to collect children's songs and have arranged them for violin. I am planning on publishing this book/CD in 2011.

In 1988, we rented a house in Turgeau, which we later purchased in 1990. In the summer of 1991, we wanted Victoria to start school, but the insecurity level and the political instability was at its height. From January 1988 to December 1990, every few weeks we had a new president. Finally, Haiti had a democratic election and a president was chosen by the people. He was Jean Bertrand Aristide. Aristide was one of the most intelligent and well-educated Haitians I've ever known. He was born in 1953 in Port Salut, a beautiful town on Haiti's southern coast. His father, a small farmer, died when he was three months old. His mother moved the family to Port-au-Prince, seeking a better life for her two children.

At the age of five, Aristide started school with priests of the Salesian order. He was further educated at the College Notre Dame in Cap-Haitian, graduating with honors in 1974. He then took a course of novitiate studies in La Vega, Dominican Republic, before returning to Haiti to study philosophy at the Grand Séminaire Notre Dame, and psychology at the State University of Haiti. After completing his post-graduate studies in 1979, Aristide traveled in Europe, studying in Italy, Greece, and Israel.

Aristide returned to Haiti in 1982 for his ordination as a Salesian priest. He was appointed curate of a small parish in Port-au-Prince. For most of his life, Haiti was ruled by the repressive dictatorships of François and Jean Claude Duvalier. The misery endured by Haiti's poor made a deep impression on Aristide, and he became an outspoken critic of Duvalierism. This included the hierarchy of the country's church, since a 1966 Vatican Concordat granted Duvalier the power to appoint Haiti's bishops. Aristide was against the rich class, known as "la bourgeoisie," the Duvalier regime, known as the "Macoutes,"; he was also anti American government, and the hierarchy of the Catholic church.

By 1985, as popular opposition to Duvalier's regime grew, Aristide was back preaching in Haiti. His inflammatory Easter

Week sermon, "A Call to Holiness," delivered at the Cathedral of Port-au-Prince and later broadcast throughout Haiti, proclaimed, "The path of those Haitians who reject the regime is the path of righteousness and love."

Aristide became a leading figure in the "ti legliz movement" for "little church." In September 1985, he was appointed to St. Jean Bosco Church, in a poor neighborhood in Port-au-Prince. Struck by the absence of young people in the church, Aristide began to organize youth, sponsoring weekly youth masses. He founded an orphanage for urban street children in 1986, called *Lafanmi Selavi* [Family is Life]. Its program sought to be a model of participatory democracy for the children it served.

As he became a leading voice for the aspirations of Haiti's dispossessed, Aristide inevitably became a target for attack. He survived at least four assassination attempts. The most widely publicized attempt, at St. Jean Bosco, occurred in September, 1988, when over one hundred armed Tonton Macoutes, wearing red armbands, forced their way into St. Jean Bosco as Aristide began Sunday mass.

As army troops and police stood by, the men fired machine guns at the congregation and attacked fleeing parishioners with machetes. Aristide's church was burned to the ground. Thirteen people are reported to have been killed, and seventy-seven wounded. Aristide survived and went into hiding. Subsequently, Salesian officials ordered Aristide to leave the country, but ten thousand Haitians protested, blocking his access to the airport.

In December 1988, Aristide was expelled from his Salesian order. A statement prepared in Rome called the priest's political activities an "incitement to hatred and violence," out of line with his role as a clergyman. Aristide appealed the decision, saying,

"The crime of which I stand accused is the crime of preaching food for all men and women." In a January 1988 interview, he said, "The solution is revolution, first in the spirit of the gospel; Jesus could not accept people going hungry. It is a conflict between classes, rich and poor."

In 1994, Aristide left the priesthood, ending years of tension with the church over his criticism of its hierarchy and his espousal of liberation theology. He married Mildred Trouillot, a US citizen, the following year. They have two daughters.

Following the violence at the aborted national elections of 1987, the 1990 elections were approached with caution. Aristide announced his candidacy for the presidency and following a six-week campaign, during which he dubbed his followers the "Front National pour le Changement et la Démocratie" (National Front for Change and Democracy) or "FNCD," the "little priest" was elected President in 1990, with 67% of the vote.

What a day! It was total joy on the streets on the day following the elections. Thousands of people were celebrating. The day of Haiti's liberation had come. Aristide was the final hope of the people. On February 7th 1991, he was elected President of Haiti. He was Haiti's first democratically elected president.

However, just eight months into his presidency he was overthrown by a truly bloody military coup. He was accused of trying to establish a dictatorship using violence and terror.

During Aristide's short-lived first period in office, he attempted to carry out substantial reforms, which brought passionate opposition from Haiti's business and military elite. He sought to bring the military under civilian control, retiring the Commander-in-Chief of the army, Hérard Abraham. He initiated investigations of human rights violations, and brought to trial several

Tontons Macoutes who had not fled the country. He also banned the emigration of many well-known Haitians until their bank accounts had been examined.

His relationship with the National Assembly soon deteriorated, and he attempted repeatedly to bypass it on judicial, cabinet, and ambassadorial appointments. His nomination of his close friend and political ally, René Préval, as Prime Minister, provoked severe criticism from political opponents who were overlooked, and the National Assembly threatened a no-confidence vote against Préval in August 1991. This led to a crowd of at least 2000 at the National Palace, which threatened violence; together with Aristide's supporters.

In September 1991, the army performed a coup against him led by Army General, Raoul Cédras, who ironically had been promoted by Aristide in June to Commander-in-Chief of the army. Aristide was deposed on September 30th, 1991. That same evening, he was sent into exile, his life saved only by the intervention of French and Venezuelan diplomats.

Aristide spent his exile first in Venezuela and then in the United States, working hard to develop international support. A United Nations trade embargo during Aristide's exile, intended to force the coup leaders to step down, was a strong blow to Haiti's already weak economy. President George H.W. Bush granted an exemption from the embargo to many US companies doing business in Haiti, and President Bill Clinton extended this exemption.

Under US and international pressure (including United Nations Security Council Resolution 940, on July 31st, 1994), the military regime backed down and US troups were deployed in the country by President Bill Clinton. On October 15th, 1994,

Aristide returned to Haiti to complete his term in office. Aristide disbanded the Haitian army, and established a civilian police force.

Aristide's first term ended in February 1996, and the constitution did not allow him to serve consecutive terms. There was some dispute over whether Aristide, prior to new elections, should serve the three years he had lost in exile, or whether his term in office should instead be counted strictly according to the date of his inauguration; it was decided that the latter should be the case.

Réné Préval, a prominent ally of Aristide and Prime Minister in 1991 under Aristide, ran during the 1995 presidential electionand took 88% of the vote. It is reported that there was about 25% participation in these elections. As mentioned above, though we had President Aristide who was democratically elected in December 1990 and ascended to power in February 1991, the situation was anything but stable. He was becoming very unpopular in the army, the Catholic clergy, and the elite class.

Consequently, Sherry and I decided to order an English program where Victoria would be home schooled. Two other parents joined us. Victoria and the two other students were the first class in The Victorian School. We were supposed to start school on September 30th,1991, when a major coup d'état orchestrated by the army sent President Aristide away to Venezuela, and we were not able to begin school until January 1992.

I also inaugurated a new musical institution entitled: "Fondation Haitienne pour le development de la Music Classique" or FHDMC,translated as: "Haitian Foundation for the Development of Classical Music" in June 1991. Its mission, identical to the mission of the new organization that I have created, "Friends of

Music Education for Haiti," was to promote music education and instrumental training to the children of Haiti. Though from its inception to 1995, it was a very successful program, as soon as I started the organization, I ran into trouble with Sister Ann Marie, Director and Founder of Holy Trinity Philharmonic Orchestra.

She felt my time working at Holy Trinity, St. Vincent's School, and the Ecole National des Arts was enough, and I was not to start my own institution. She told me that the Holy Trinity music program was the only one that had, and would, survive the test of time in Haiti, and all the others would crumble.

I tried to explain to her that I would still continue working for Holy Trinity -- her wonderful music program where I had been a student since 1972, and was at that time an instructor. I further explained to her that it was in the best interest of her program where for the only Philharmonic Orchestra in Haiti to grow, because it and St. Vincent's School were my life's musical references, and if she tried to destroy other musical institutions like mine, eventually her own efforts of the past years would be destroyed as well. After all, Holy Trinity would never have room to musically satisfy the needs of all these parents who were asking for music lessons.

Unfortunately, I was right. The January earthquake has destroyed the music school, including the concert hall, and now there is no music hall for any professional or non-professional performance in Haiti. Had other programs been allowed to survive, perhaps in spite of the earthquake, the situation wouldn't be so grim as it is now.

I added that she needed to perceive her music program as a tree, and the other musical institutions that derived from hers as branches of that tree. Her role was to support my program or any program of her professional musicians in the future; not to destroy them, as was the case for "Vision Nouvelle," a music program which was created by Yves-Rose Phillipe-Auguste later than mine, and which Sister Ann Marie never supported either.

Her response was, "I wish these institutions as well as yours good luck." Then, sponsors that had supported my music foundation called to let me know that, much to my dismay, Sister Ann Marie called them and asked them not to sponsor my program any further. We ran into so many problems. For example, many teachers that I tried to hire, or musicians I asked to play with my students, were afraid that Sister Ann Marie would retaliate if they worked for my foundation. Holy Trinity had the only acceptable concert hall in Haiti, which could hold about 470 people, and there were many rules to prevent me or other people who had music programs from renting it. I was like a horrible black sheep among the musicians.

I finally had enough when one evening in 1995, in one of her speeches to the members of the orchestra, she told them that I was a bad example not to be followed. So, in June 1995, at the end of the foundation's last concert, I announced that FHDMC was officially closed. At that time, the FHDMC had about 120 students. I simply told myself that I hoped I would live long enough to restart it again in the future or something similar to it.

On April 3rd, 1992, Bradley was born. Sherry's time in labor for Bradley was longer than Victoria's; about thirteen hours, due to the fact that she was given the wrong medication to induce labor. It wasn't a fun experience as it was for Victoria's birth, because Sherry's doctor had simultaneously three women in labor in different hospitals, and he was driving from one hospital to the next, managing the three mothers. At times, it was simply horrifying. When the doctor realized it was getting late (and in those days, no one stayed out after dark), he used an IV needle to break Sherry's water and speed up the birth process. Happily, all ended well for Bradley and Sherry.

In the meantime, by 1994, the political situation had worsened. General Cedras was the only person in charge. After Marc Bazin was removed as Prime Minister by the army, the country had no head of state until the arrival of the American Marines. Life was hard. A gallon of gasoline varied between $30 ht to $100 ht. The country was preparing for war with the United States Marines and we were all scared. After hours of negotiations, the Marines were able to come in without any resistance from the Haitian army. Then President Aristide, who was returned to Haiti by President Clinton, stayed in power for a while and President Préval became the next president.

René Garcia Préval was born in "Marmelade Cap-Haitian," on January 17th, 1943. He studied business at the College of Gembloux and the University of Leuven in Belgium, and also studied biology at the University of Pisa in Italy. Préval's father, also an agronomist, had risen to the position of Minister of Agriculture in the government of Général Paul Magloire, the predecessor of Duvalier. Leaving Haiti because his political past presented him as a potential opponent, Préval's father found work with UN agencies in Africa.

His political party was "Lespwa" which means "hope." He married Guerda Géri Benoit, divorced her, then married Solange Lafontant. In 2009, he married Elisabeth Delatour and they are still married today.

After spending five years in Brooklyn, New York, occasionally working as a restaurant waiter, Préval returned to Haiti and obtained a position with the National Institute for Mineral Resources. Préval was very much involved in the agricultural workings of society. After a few years, he opened a bakery in Port-au-Prince with some business partners. While operating his company, he continued to be active in political circles and charity work, such as providing bread to the orphanage of Salesian Father Jean Bertrand Aristide, with whom he developed a close relationship.

After the election of Aristide as president in 1990, Préval served as his Prime Minister from February 13th to October 11th, 1991, going into exile following the September 30th, 1991 military coup. In 1996, Préval was elected as president for a five-year term, with 88% of the popular vote. Upon his 1996 inauguration, Préval became the second democratically elected head of state in the country's 200-year history. In 2001, he became the second President of Haiti to leave office as a result of the natural expiration of an uninterrupted term, the first being General Nissage Saget, president from 1869 to 1874.

As president, Préval instituted a number of economic reforms, most notably the privatization of various government companies. By the end of Préval's term, the unemployment rate (though still quite high) had fallen to its lowest level since the fall of Duvalier. Préval also instituted an aggressive program of agrarian reform in Haiti's countryside. His presidency, however, was also marked by fierce political clashes with a parliament dominated by opposition party members (OPL) and an increasingly vocal Fanmi Lavalas (party of the former president), which opposed the structural adjustment and privatization program of Préval's government.

As president, Préval was a strong supporter of investigations and trials related to human rights violations committed by military and police personnel. Préval dissolved the parliament in 1999 and ruled by decree for the duration of the final year of his presidency.

Préval ran again as the "Lespwa" candidate in the Haitian presidential election. The election took place after nearly two years of international peacekeeping, which some described as an unelected dictatorship. Partial election results, released on February 9th, indicated that he had won with about 60% of the vote, but as further results were released, his share of the vote slipped to 48.7% – thus making a run-off necessary.

Several days of popular demonstrations in favor of Préval followed in Port-au-Prince and other cities in Haiti. On February 14th, Préval claimed that there had been fraud among the vote counts, and demanded that he be declared the winner outright of the first round. Protesters paralyzed the capital with burning barricades and stormed a luxury hotel — Hotel Montana located in the affluent suburb of Petionville — to demand results from Haiti's nearly week-old election as ex-President René Préval fell further below the 50% needed to win the presidency.

By the way, this beautiful hotel was destroyed by the earthquake. I am glad I was able to spend time there with Myslie, especially for the December 31st 2008 gala with the group "New Look," performing.

On February 16th, 2006, Préval was declared the winner of the presidential election by the Provisional Electoral Council with 51.15% of the vote, after the exclusion of "blank" ballots from the count.

He was sworn in on May 14th, following Haiti's legislative run-off vote in April. He could not be sworn in until a sitting

Parliament was in place. When he was sworn in, Préval emphasized the importance of unity, saying that division was Haiti's "main problem" and that Haitians had to "work together."

Préval drew much of his support from Haiti's poorest people; he was especially widely supported in the poorest neighborhoods of Port-au-Prince. However, many of the poor demanded that the former President Aristide be allowed to return and that civil enterprise workers fired by the Latortue government be reinstated. This caused increasing tension in the slums of Port-au-Prince.

Préval promised to build a massive road system which would boost trade and transportation around the country. Since Preval's induction, the economy has seen a sizeable increase.

Back to my story. Though the New Victorian School was doing well, my life with Sherry started to get complicated. Beginning around 1989, the relationship started to go sour. We gradually couldn't agree on anything. Couple this with the closing of FHDMC; on August 1995, I moved to Miami. This decision was difficult because I had to leave Victoria, who was seven years old, and Bradley then three years old, behind. Nevertheless it had to be done.

In September, when I arrived in Miami, I first stayed with Jolius Tinhomme. He was one of my friends since childhood at the boys' dormitory. I worked part time in two Baptist churches and gave some private music lessons. Then Onickel made the necessary arangement in January 1996 for me to rent a basement-like apartment at one of his friends' houses. Also, in February, I was employed by the Miami Dade County Public Schools "MDCPS" as a substitute teacher teaching music in grades one through five in Opa Locka and Palm Lakes Elementary Schools.

THE MIRACLE OF MUSIC

When I started teaching in Opa Locka, my assumption was that it would be like teaching children in Haiti. They would automatically sit, listen, and learn. But I was way off. It was something that I would never imagine. The children's behavior was horrible. They wouldn't do anything I asked them to do, and they were walking everywhere in the classroom. I simply couldn't teach them anything. I kept on sending them to the office and the administrators kept on sending them back to me, telling me that it wasn't not their job to discipline the children; it was up to me to control their behavior. When they came back to class from the office, they behaved even worse.

I had no idea what was happening, and I thought of leaving the public school system. But a voice inside of me kept on telling me that I needed the experience, and that I should stay. So, I managed as best as could, and was happy when school was over in June.

Palm Lakes Elementary was much more pleasant. The children were wonderful and I had few discipline problems. What I found was that the more control the principal teacher had over the class, the better the children behaved for the substitute teacher. In addition, I had the support of the primary teachers in Palm Lakes, as well as the assistant principal and the principal. It was an excellent school where I would really love to work if I were to stay longer in MDCPS.

I decided to stay in MDCPS for a while in order to learn the functioning of the school system; however, the teacher that I had replaced returned from her maternity leave and assumed her job; consequently, I had to look for another school.

On February 28th, 1996, I requested a meeting with a group of my friends and with their assistance and collaboration, I founded

"Haitian Corporation for Musical Development," or HCMD. It was inaugurated in a concert in March. Its mission was to initiate Haitian children in Dade, Monroe, Broward and Palm Beach counties into classical music through music classes. We started classes on October 1996, and we had a weekly radio program to motivate the parents to sign up their children for music lessons.

The music program grew to about ninety students. On May 1999, we organized the first Walenstein Annual Music competition for youth and young adults ages twelve to twenty-one. The competition took place at the Omni Colonade Hotel in Coral Gables, and it was a true success. We also opened the music program to other comunities of the counties where we served.

Also in September 1996, I decided to give my relationship with Sherry a second chance. So Victoria, Bradley and Sherry moved to North Miami. Victoria went to Charles Drew Elementary for one quarter, and was transferred to Gratigny Elementary. Bradley was homeschooled for a while, because when Sherry traveled to Haiti, Bradley went along with her. Then Bradley went to Gratigny Elementary School as well.

As difficult as the experience was to work in the public school, I figured I should stay longer in order to have a better knowledge of the American school system which would benefit the New Victorian School. Consequently I applied in different schools around Miami Dade and I received a call from Jose Marti Middle School for an interview. I went and I was approved to teach strings and guitar. Coming from Haiti, I knew nothing of the public school system except the little experience I had as a substitute. But now I was going to become a full-time teacher.

I worked at Jose Marti from August 1996 through June 1998. It was like spending two years in hell. The amount of paperwork that I had to do was unbelievable to me. When I got there, there were very few musical instruments in the classroom, and 6th, 7th and 8th grade students were mixed for music class. The 6th graders would fight constantly with the older 7th and 8th graders.

Because I couldn't see well, the students would be throwing papers everywhere, and by the end of the day, the classroom was a mess. They wrote profanities on the instruments, the chairs, the walls, and the doors. Many of the students lived on the streets and were gang members; thus, they were very violent -- in short, the level of bad behavior was far worse than at Opa Locka Elementary School.

The problem of classroom management was also in my lap. I didn't know any of the administrative rules that would help me better manage the classroom. That made my life difficult because the children knew them. For example, I would send a child with bad behavior with a blank referral. And of course the assistant principal wouldn't know what to do with the student.

When the students were done with the work I gave them to do, I would send them out early as opposed to waiting for the bell to ring, or if there was a special event, I would drop them in the auditorium and leave. Then the students at the end of the event couldn't get their book bags in my room to go home. So for the first weeks on the job, I received several letters of reprimand for violations of school rules.

I would have never survived the system without the valuable assistance of Ms. Jessica Napolis, who was the keyboard and choral instructor, and Ms. Patricia Porter, who was the drama instructor. They were my guardian angels. They taught me the rules, helped me avoid difficult situations with the students, and gave me advice on how to handle certain administrative situations.

By the second year, (1997/1998), I had more experience and had fewer problems with the students. But I still find it amazing that any teacher, blind or full-sighted, is able to survive the public school system without being fired or worse, sent to prison. One of the major problems teachers face in the public school system is the immeasurable power that is given to the students. Their words are always believed by everyone. They seem to have all the rights and the teachers have none. The students are innocent until proven guilty and the teachers are guilty until proven innocent.

To illustrate this point: one day a student wanted to go to lunch ten minutes early, and I told him no. In the afternoon, Ms. Alonzo, one of the assistant principals, told me that I had an important parent meeting the next day. When I came in the morning, she told me that the meeting was no longer necessary. What happened was that the child was angry due to the fact I didn't let him go out to lunch early, and he took some kind of marker, and colored his white skin. When he arrived home, he told his mother that I badly scratched him. His mother then called the school asking for a meeting. Later, when the father came home, the mother called him to see what I had done to his son. But luckily for me, the child had washed his arm and the "evidence" no longer existed.

Another situation, even worse than the first, occurred one day while I was showing a movie, and a student in another class wanted to see it. When I saw he was there and didn't belong in my class, I ran after him. He flew out the door and my left hand hit the wall and there was a cut on my finger. So the friend who brought him to my class told the student to file a report, saying that I hit him to the point where my finger was cut .Obviously the proof was there since my finger was cut. But it was cut from the wall, and not by beating up the student. The parent of the child reported the incident to the school, the principal called the union representative, and I got a warning not to beat up the children.

I wasn't going to stay long in MDCPS, because I had my own school. However, what really made me leave the public school early was that one Friday afternoon; I locked my door and left the school. When I came back on Monday morning, I was scheduled to have an observation by an assistant principal. But my personal stereo was gone. So I went to the assistant principal, Ms. Fisher, and reported the loss. She told me to get another radio at the library to do the presentation. But the radios at the library were very small; that was why I brought my personal stereo to school.

So I went to Mr. Enriquez, the school principal, and reported the situation. Mr. Enriquez looked at me and said, "What do you want me to do about it? Do you want me to go to K-mart and buy you one?" I exploded, telling him that even as a principal, his comment was rude, uncalled-for, and inconsiderate. I had a board in my hand; I dropped it on the floor and left. Mr. Enriquez screamed saying, "That's unprofessional." Sherry, who was behind me, picked up the board and took it to the classroom.

Class started at 8:50. The students arrived, and I was crying. They asked me what was wrong. I explained to the story to them. One girl said, "Mr. Joseph, if you want I can help you get the radio back. It's the janitor who stole it. Just say the word."

Then all the students responded, "Yes. We can find it for you."

I told them, "Thank you, but that's okay. I don't want to get you people into trouble."

For once it felt wonderful. All the students were nice to me all day. I didn't have to worry about any discipline problems, at least for that day. At about 9:05, Ms. Napolis came to my room. "Mr. Joseph, you are not alone. They stole my CD player and some other items."

As she was talking, Dana, the band teacher came in. "They also stole my stereo."

Ms. Porter came in, saying, "They stole a bunch a things in my room that we used for props." We talked for a while and they left.

The students in my class were furious. Thirty minutes later, Mr. Enriquez sent for me. I went downstairs to his office still crying. When I arrived, I found Ms. Fisher, the union representative, and the principal, Mr. Enriquez. I knew then I was in big trouble. He spoke first saying, "I called you downstairs because your behavior was unprofessional, reprehensible, and unacceptable."

Ms. Fisher said, "I did tell you to go to the library and get another radio, didn't I?"

I said, "Yes, you did, but they are too small for music; they don't have enough bass."

Ms. Fisher said, "It doesn't matter. You didn't follow my order as your assistant principal."

I said, "I am sorry about that; but the small library radios cannot be used in my classroom. That's why I brought my own personal stereo."

The union representative said, "The union will not be able to protect you if you continue being unprofessional."

I said, "The person had no right to go to my room during the weekend and steal my radio."

Mr. Enriquez said, "It doesn't matter whether or not someone stole your radio in your room. As long as the radio is lost in your room, it's your fault; your own responsibility."

I got really angry. "You mean if I lock the door on a Friday afternoon, go home, come back on Monday and find something missing in my room, it's my fault?" That was of course a trick question.

Mr. Enriquez replied, "Sure it's your fault. After all it's your room; and all that is in it is under your responsibility."

I said, "Well then, the whole floor is guilty."

Mr. Enriquez said, "What do you mean?"

I replied, "Mr. Enriquez, Ms. Napolis and Dana lost their stereos, Ms. Porter lost several items in her rooms, and I lost my stereo. I guess we are just guilty and irresponsible teachers."

Mr. Enriquez was in shock! "What?" he said.

The union representative said, "I think you have a problem upstairs."

I said, "Can I leave?"

Mr. Enriquez said, "Yes, you can." Then I left feeling VERY happy. If only my stereo was stolen, I would have received a letter of reprimand and probably I would have been fired for being disrespectful and insubordinate to my superiors.

In June 1998, I gave my letter of resignation to the school administrators. As troublesome as these two years were, I was able to learn so much of the positive and negative aspects of the Miami-Dade school system which helped me tremendously in managing the New Victorian School, which is known in Port-au-Prince as one of the most disciplined academic institutions, by creating a balance of power between the administrators, the teachers, and the students; as opposed to the students having all the power.

As mentioned above, for family unity, I did ask Sherry and the children to come to Miami. My hope was after a year of Sherry and me being apart, that absence would have helped the relationship. But it got worse. The arguments were more constant than in Haiti, and we were drifted apart in terms of interests and life philosophies. The Christmas seasons were still horrible, and our social life was totally stagnant. As we arrived at a new century, I felt like something would have to be changed in the family.

Two of my December 31st, 1999, resolutions for the new century were to spend all my future Christmases in Haiti, and to go to all the places and countries that I ever wanted to visit.

6

(2000-2010) Back in Haiti at the New Victorian School, divorce, new wife

I was really happy on January 1st, 2000, at midnight to see the new year and the new century, because I was a little worried that the world would end that night. Sherry, Victoria, Bradley, and I were at Bayside Market Place located in downtown Miami, watching the fireworks. I was looking forward to a new century of hard work and lots of fun. However, on January 12th, around 4:30 p.m., I received a call from Tania Desamours, who was then one of my best friends in Haiti. She told me that The Victorian School was on fire.

Sherry and I made the necessary arangements for the children, and we went to Haiti the next day. There was nothing left of the school. So I started right away with the cleaning up of the rubble and within two weeks, we managed to continue with the school year. With the financial assistance of many friends, we were able to rebuild the school under the name The **NEW** Victorian School. It was a much more modern construction, less susseptible to fire. The construction of the school was completed in the summer of 2001.

I decided to spend more time in Haiti to take care of the school while Sherry worked full time at Barry University, then Miami Dade College. Bradley was still at Gratigny Elementary and Victoria was in Horace Mann Middle School. Victoria continued learning the violin, and Bradley, the piano.

In December 2000, I spent my first Christmas in Haiti since 1979. I learned from one of my best friends, the late Ariel Dunwell, who was also my piano student, that there was an annual gala every 31st of December at Kinam 2 Hotel. I figured I would go and check it out. It was the most magnificent night I've ever had. It was hard to believe that I was in Haiti. Everyone was super-dressed. Each table had the name of the people to be seated, and had all kind of drinks.

I believe that night Strings and Zin were the musical groups selected for that particular event. They had a gourmet buffet at midnight, fireworks, and Soupe Joumou -- "pumpkin soup" -- around 4:00 a.m. Since then, I have been going to that party every year; except in 2010, when I went to listen to Djaz des Jeunes and Septantrional, two ancient groups, that I used to hear only on the radio when I was a child, and I wanted to hear them live.

For the next five years, from 2000 through 2005, I continued structuring the HCMD in Miami, managing The New Victorian School in Haiti, teaching, and performing concerts in Haiti and Miami. In addition, I used the music software program "Finale" to update the four volumes of instructional methods for strings that I started in 1983. I wrote music for an album called: "A violin in love," and a religious album. I never had time to put them on CD. Now they will become my projects for the coming years.

THE MIRACLE OF MUSIC

Early in 2005, we legally changed the name of Haitian Foundation for Musical Development to Walenstein Musical Organization, and modified the program so that it would become all-inclusive. The program included: a concert series for children and youth, master classes, seminars, workshops, and an annual music competition. In October 2007, we inaugurated the Walenstein Symphony Orchestra, which was at first part of The Walenstein Musical Organization; in January 2010, it became an independent 501(c)(3) organization. Its mission is to offer quality professional concerts and to work with students of the Walenstein Musical Organization.

In September 2008, one of my childhood dreams was realized. The Walenstein Symphony Orchestra had its first concert, entitled: "A Romantic Evening with Tchaikovsky," where three of Tchaikovsky's major works were performed: *Capriccio Italian, Rococo Variations for Cello and Orchestra,* and *Symphony No. 6.*

In the meantime, my relationship with Sherry continued to fall apart. We were no longer compatible. However, I felt that Bradley and Victoria were too young to put them through a divorce. So, the next best thing was to stay in Haiti as long as I could and spend less time in Miami.

By September 2003, though still legally married, we were pretty much separated. Thus, I started dating a new Haitian girl in Haiti, Edna. She was very beautiful, sociable, and practical. She loved to go out and have fun. We would spend lots of time at South Beach, Disney World, and the like.

On April 2006, I received a call from a friend telling me about a cruise line that had a fourteen-day special from Miami to Europe for $500 per person and $500 more per person to fly coming back from Madrid to Miami. That was a total of $1,000 per person. This trip was a dream come true. Since my encounter with the Tchaikovsky album in 1972, I always wanted to visit Rome, to see the Sistine chapel, and the Vatican. Tchaikovsky went there for a visit and was totally inspired.

However, I had a problem -- Sherry not only didn't like to go out with me, but also hated cruises. But there was no way I was going to miss this once in a lifetime opportunity. So I asked Edna if she would like to go and she said yes. So we took the cruise, visiting several cities in Portugal, France, and Italy. It was a true dream vacation. When Sherry found out about me traveling with Edna, though she didn't have the details, she was furious. We had one last huge argument, and the relationship ended. On September 18th, 2006, we were officially divorced. Victoria stayed in Miami with Sherry, and I took Bradley with me to Haiti where he stayed for two years (2006-2008).

In November 2006, after a series of arguments, Edna and I also broke up. It was as if my social and love life were falling completely apart. Then I made the decision to look online for a date. Through a company, I found a date: Debbie from Canada. We spent almost a year dating before we realized that it wasn't going to work out due to conflict of interests. I dated several more girls whom I met online but nothing worked out. So in June 2008, Myslie, who was a student in the New Victorian School secretarial program from 2005 to 2007, was my next and last date. We were engaged in August 2009, and were married on October 1st, 2009.

THE MIRACLE OF MUSIC

She was pretty much the woman I was looking for -- depend-able, reliable, talented, pleasing, and highly logical. Myslie was ex-cellent in communication, loved going out to nightclubs or any-where else, and detested arguing. In addition, since 2003, I had constant problems with my feet, particularly the right one. And by January 2006, the right foot had developed what are called "varicose veins." My right foot was dying while I was still much alive (necrosis). This problem might have resulted from spending hours and hours practicing the violin standing up. I must have seen at least five different doctors, spending thousands of dollars in Haiti with little result. Myslie started taking care of my feet and they became perfectly fine. The last doctor I saw in January 2010 before her death told her to keep doing whatever she was doing.

Because of the damage my right foot sustained during the earthquake, the varicose veins situation has started again, particularly since July 2010. Except this time, because my right foot was under tremendous pressure under the rubble, the condition is worse than before -- and this time, I am not going to find Myslie to fix it. She was studying cosmetology in order to open her own beauty salon in September 2010. At twenty-six years of age, after years of studying, her dreams were going to come true: having her own business, and traveling around the world.

7

The Notorious Earthquake, My Little Tomb

On December 31st, 2009, happily married, Myslie and I went to Djaz des Jeunes, one of my favorite groups during my childhood, as well as Septantrional. She had her New Year's resolutions, which were to start her own beauty salon, to visit Europe, and to have a public wedding on December 18th, 2010. She started looking for her wedding dress online and we were making all kinds of wedding plans.

My New Year's resolutions were to legally make Walenstein Symphony Orchestra (WSO) independent from Walenstein Musical Organization. That did materialize on January 6th, 2010, when WSO became a 501 (c)(3) institution under IRS tax exempt status. In addition, I wanted to expand The New Victorian School French section to Philo, which is twelfth grade, and expand the music program. I was also looking forward to my public wedding with Myslie and our European trip. But as they say in Haiti, "L'homme propose, Dieu dispose." meaning "Man proposes, God decides." I would never have imagined that an earthquake would come and change my wonderful stable world.

On January 12th, 2010, I awoke before 7 a.m. to a cloudy day. It was a day like any other winter day in Haiti's capital, Port-au-Prince. When I opened my eyes, I had a Christian song in my head that I'd learned many years ago when I went to St. Vincent's School for Handicapped Children. The lyrics are in Creole, but roughly translated the refrain goes, "Oh Lord, hold me more firmly, for if I slip and fall down, oh Lord, I will have no life."

For some reason, that tune stayed with me all day. My wife, Myslie, was already about. Dressed in white, which was the uniform of her school, she put her hand on my shoulder, gave me a kiss and an affectionate squeeze, which I returned, and she went to her cosmetology class as she had been doing since September 2009. Myslie had the same dreams for three consecutive nights: January 9th, 10th, and 11th. She told me that she dreamed her mother's house was on fire. I told her it was nothing, and she should just pray to God for her family's safety. Unfortunately, I never made the connection between her dreams and The Victorian School fire of January 12th, 2000 until I was under the ground.

We were still newlyweds, married only three months. Although only half my age, at only twenty-six, Myslie had taught me so much about love and women, knowledge that had long eluded me, and now made me consistently happy for the first time in a long time. She was also seven months pregnant with our son, whose name was going to be Guastafesti Joseph.

Amazingly enough, a few days before the earthquake, she had a chance to go to her doctor for a sonogram, and spent quite some time watching our son yawning, with his little hand in his mouth, and sucking. Unbeknownst to her, this wonderful moment would be the last time she would see her son. She had managed her pregnancy perfectly and was never sick or overweight.

Since the beginning of December 2009, every night, Myslie would listen to particular works of Mozart for two hours. I had selected them based on the theory of the Mozart Effect which stipulates that children should listen to Mozart's music during pregnancy. It stimulates the brain, and relaxes both mother and child. In addition, since October 2009, I started giving her piano lessons and she practiced diligently for thirty minutes every evening. She had her last lesson on January 10th, 2010, performing pieces from Book Three of *Step by Step,* a piano method written by Edna Mae Burnam.

I didn't have far to go to get to work, for Myslie and I lived on the school's first floor. The second floor had the computer room, a classroom, and a kitchen. The third floor had two classrooms and a guest room. The fourth floor had three classrooms. The fifth floor had a nice view of the ocean, but nothing else – yet.

I had a lot to do that day, including a full schedule of music lessons and parent meetings. I also had to complete a financial statement for the IRS for my non-profit 501(c)(3) musical institution, the Walenstein Musical Organization, located in Miami, Florida. The work had taken a year to complete and my secretary wanted to e-mail it to my daughter, Victoria, who lived in Miami, but our Internet connection had broken.

The secretary called the repairman, who came at 11 a.m. He did some preliminary tests, then told me that he had to do some more tests in order to find the problem. I asked him to explain the test he was going to perform, which he did, for the problem was on our end. Strangely enough, he offered to do the testing.

But I told him I would do the test myself later. He insisted, saying, "Since I am here, I may as well do it for you."

I told him, "It's okay, the test is easy to do, and I will do it later." This decision to not let him do the test would save my life.

Myslie also had lots to do. School. Banking. Grocery shopping. I planned to spend the evening with my best friend, Onickel Augustin. He lived in Miami but had come to visit and was staying in our third-floor guest room. We'd met years ago at the St. Vincent's School for Handicapped in Port-au-Prince. I was nine; he was a few years older. Like me, he was also blind. And a musician. For some reason, he took me under his wing and introduced me to the violin.

I finished giving my last lesson at 4:30 p.m. to one of my most talented students, Sarah Colimon. I walked her to the gate, walked back to the now empty school, and found Myslie sitting in the middle of our apartment, reading. I sat down in front of my computer to do some work. But immediately, I felt restless. I didn't want to stay in my room.

"Myslie," I said, "I'm going upstairs to see Onickel. I have a message from the Internet repairman for a test we can do in order for it to work well. Would you like to come and help us?"

"No, no, " she said, in a low, dark tone of voice as she turned the page. "I am reading something."

"Are you sure?"

"Yes. I am studying." Myslie explained to Ms. Lubin, my principal administrative assistant for the school, that she was really tired from her errands, and, of course, from being so pregnant.

"Okay," I said. "I'll be right back."

Onickel was upstairs in the guest room with some friends. To get there I had to use our outside staircase – just as the children did every day – to reach the balcony. Each floor had one that ran the length of the building. On one side were the rooms; on the other an iron railing. If you fell over the railing you'd end up in the school's yard below. But no one could fall. The iron was very strong and all the children were very careful.

Each room had two doors: one screened and one wooden. I opened both and found Onickel inside, deep in a heated debate with four of his friends, about God and the Bible. I spent a few minutes listening and thought, "This argument will have no end; I'll go back downstairs and work, and return later." I was too tired to join in. I turned around and took a few steps toward the door. Suddenly I heard a deep, dark rumbling, and the building began to shake. Violently. The floor rolled up and down under my feet. I screamed, "Oh, my God!" I grabbed the door frame. Onickel yelled, "Earthquake!" What happened next took far less time than it will for you to read these next words.

For a split second I thought about what I should do. I thought the shaking would stop after a few seconds. I'd just stay by the door and when it was over, I'd walk out. My only experience with an earthquake had been a small one in 2004. I was with my ex-girlfriend, Edna, in our room, when I heard some plates going clink-clink-clink and wondered if there were mice. I didn't know it was a quake until I saw the ceiling light moving. We both ran outside. But this was such a minor earthquake that no one even talked about it on the news.

Also, I was standing in the new addition to the school, which was made of cement blocks filled with iron rebar and cement. Very solid by Haitian standards. I don't know if there are building codes in Haiti like there are in America. You just have your engineer verify the architect's plan, you build, and you're done. No one builds something to fall down.

Instead of stopping, as I'd hoped, the floor and the door kept moving. I couldn't run, or move, because of the shaking. And I was on the third floor. Even a sighted person would have done what I did: hold on and wait it out. Besides, God forbid if the worst happened and the fifth floor fell on the fourth, and the fourth on the third: at least the doorway, with its heavy beam frame, would be the safest place.

I was wrong. Suddenly, the doorway disappeared. It was as if someone had been standing next to me, said a magic word, and then suddenly vanished. Then the floor underneath me disintegrated, and like Wile E. Coyote in the in Roadrunner cartoons, I stood on nothing. The ground opened up and I lost conciousness.

A while later, I woke up. I heard only silence. My eyes watered from the dust. Though my left artificial eye is gone, my right eye can still sense light and shadow, but I saw nothing. As if in a dream I asked, "Where am I?" No answer. I asked myself, "Is this for real? I must be asleep, having a nightmare." I told myself: "Try to wake up!" I tried to wake up. That's when I felt the awful pain. This was no dream.

I lay on my stomach on some iron bars, which were the balcony railing. When I tried to move I discovered that my right foot was locked tight and burned as if the skin had been sheared off with sandpaper. I could inch it a tiny bit to the left, which lessened the pressure, but it didn't help all that much.

My other foot was loose but when I moved it, pain ran up my leg like a hot wire, and I felt something wet and dangling. The rest of my body hurt as if nails had been pounded into me and I was covered with dust and grime. My right hand was deeply scratched, but – oh my God – my left arm and hand were a mess. They were huge. The fingers were swollen many times their normal size and couldn't bend. I wondered if I would ever play violin again.

If only this were a dream -- but of course, it wasn't. There had been an earthquake and I was obviously buried down here beneath the school. But how far down was "down here," and what was above me? I touched the ground under me with my right hand and I could tell that I was on the yard.

An aftershock rocked the ground and I held my breath, expecting the worst. But thankfully, nothing moved – except my heartbeat, which pounded so loudly and progressively faster in my chest that I knew my already high blood pressure was soaring. I wanted *very badly* to get out, but that would never happen if I had a stroke. I had to stay calm, and control my breathing. But my mind still raced. Would I lose my feet and never be able to walk and dance "Sweet Micky" or "New Look" again -- especially for the annual ball on December 31st at Kinam Two Hotel or Caribe Hotel? Would I be blind *and* crippled? Would I ever play violin again? What had happened to Myslie? And Onickel and his friends? Was anyone else in the school? Had the whole city fallen down? Would I *live*? Why was I here?

But at least I was alive. I could have used some Flanax, though. It's equivalent to Aleve. Even though my foot was trapped, I had to try to escape. Maybe I could pull it loose, even if little by little. I couldn't just lie there, give up, and die without a fight. I'd never forgive myself. I had to do *something*. I would have liked to make a phone call and to tell someone, anyone, that I was alive. But I never carried my cell phone with me.

I stretched and slowly drew my upper body backward across

the railing into a fetal position, hunching my back. I felt a flat circular surface above me, but at least I had some room to move. I wanted to feel around the area, maybe move some blocks and find some light. Even if I couldn't get out, people would see where I was and would try to help me.

I tried to put weight on my shattered left foot. That hurt, but so what? Then my locked right foot stopped me, like a dog chained to a post, And out of nowhere I heard a voice saying, "Oh really! I find you a nice safe place to stay, and you are trying to get out? Well, good luck."

What? Who said that? I waited. Nothing. I went back to my original place and lay down again, scared. Had death spoken to me? Was it near? My concept of God had never been someone with a big stick, but a being anyone could talk to. So I talked -- babbled, really -- questioning my fate. I made no sense, and looking back I realize I was selfishly thinking only of myself, saying, "God, why did you put me here? I have always helped those in need. I didn't kill anyone. What have I done? Probably the worst thing I did was going out with a lot of girls. Is that why I'm being punished?"

I heard the voice again. "Why don't you ask *yourself* these questions?" I knew, then, that I wasn't alone. I don't mean that anyone buried nearby had spoken. The voice was in my head, but it wasn't mine. Instead, a powerful spirit rose up inside me.

"Is that you, Jesus?" I whispered, uncertain. "Who is here?"

"Yes, it is me, Jesus." But was it? Come on. I was in shock. How was this possible?

I was raised as a Catholic, and had gone to an Episcopalian school. My mother was extremely religious. We had to go to church every Sunday, and she taught us how to pray. We had to memorize Psalms 20, 23, 27, 91, and others. Onickel and I used to read the Bible a lot when we were kids. But even though I believed in God, Jesus, and the Holy Spirit, I had always felt that religion had been imposed on me. I didn't like having to get up at five o'clock in the morning to go to church. I didn't like – especially in the Catholic Church – that my knees hurt from spending so much time kneeling on a hard, wooden board. The service was too long, and when I was a child, it was in Latin.

If anything, I was a religious person from afar. That is, I admired those whom I thought were wonderful Christians, like my former violin teacher, John Jost. I did believe in John 3:16 in the Bible: "For God so loved the world that he gave his only begotten son, that whosoever believeth in him should not perish but have eternal life," which I learned as a child, but that's as far as it went. Mostly, I found religion to be a source of argument. I prayed only when I had a problem, and forgot that Jesus existed when everything was fine. I took everything he did for me for granted, and I felt proud of myself when I accomplished something. I rarely thanked him for my life's successes, and worse, I always blamed him for my failures.

So why would God come to me? I didn't know, but I couldn't argue with the voice. "Thank you for being here with me, Jesus," I said. Better safe than sorry. Jesus or not, my immediate worry was dying. My mind raced through the ways that could happen. My high blood pressure could kill me. The air could run out. An aftershock could send concrete -- especially the falling massive building behind where I was -- to crush me. The Bible says that when death is near, you need to pray and ask for forgiveness.

Clearly, I needed to pray. If I didn't pray, who knew what might happen? I didn't want to take a chance. In desperation I decided to say my last prayers. Based on everything I had learned from the various churches I used to go to, I did prepare my own prayer which I would recite before I died. So I'd memorized a set of last prayers long ago. I thanked Jesus for the opportunity to say them. After all, the block wall on my right foot could have landed on my head instead.

First, I recited "The Lord's Prayer" and "Psalm 23" in French, and asked for my sins to be forgiven. I used French because it was faster than English and I didn't know how much time I had left. I also didn't ask for "our" sins to be absolved, but my own. If this was my time, it was my problem.

"Dear Jesus, just as you forgave the prisoner on your right while you were being crucified, just as he was able to accept you as the Son of God, and it's only through you that all sins can be forgiven, I am attesting that you, Jesus, are the Son of God. I believe that God sent you as the Savior for all who believe in you, and I ask you, Lord, to forgive all my sins and ensure that the purity of my body and soul will allow me – just like that prisoner – to be with you in Paradise. Almighty God, I also forgive all who have offended me in one form or another. Bless my enemies in the name of Jesus Christ, our Lord, amen."

Then I prayed for my daughter, Victoria; my son, Bradley; my wife, Myslie and our unborn son; my ex-wife, Sherry; my friends – including Onickel; my students at the school and the Walenstein Music program in Miami. I prayed for my two beloved countries, Haiti and the US, both of which claimed me as a citizen.

Then my last prayer: "Heavenly Father, just as Jesus gave you his soul before his demise, and put it into your hands, I give you my spirit in the name of Jesus Christ our Savior, amen. Please, God Almighty, be with me as I make the transition from this world to the next. I ask you all this in the name of Jesus Christ our Savior, Amen."

Then I sang "How Great Thou Art," "God Will Take Care of You," Onward Christian Soldiers," "Amazing Grace," and "When the Row is Called Up." Honestly, I didn't know all the words, but I was sure that humming the tunes would be enough to let God and Jesus get the message that I was sincere.

Then I lay there, quiet and exhausted in the dark, peacefully waiting for death to arrive. Waiting to die is the strangest feeling; it's like you're sitting patiently for a bus to come, now and then peering down the street to see if it's in the distance. I should have been scared, but I wasn't. Despite my feelings about religion, I did believe that death is simply a transition from one kind of life to another. It's not like you're going to *really die*. I prayed that my transition would be smooth.

This was a Rosicrucian teaching. As I have stated in a previous chapter, I'd been a member for a few years when I was in New York in the eighties and been interested in mysticism. Besides, the concept of "I'm going through a transition" felt better than "I'm dying." The Rosicrucians believe in the law of vibrations -- that is, nothing stays still. Everything goes through different forms. The human is no different. It goes through evolution and devolution.

In Christianity, you die and one day, when Jesus comes, you're going to be judged. It's almost like you're sitting there for the next 500 years. Imagine those people who died 10,000 years ago. They're still sitting, waiting for the Judgment Day.

I think it's easy to understand why I liked *transition* better. It's just like the corn my father used to grow. You transform it into cornmeal, and many other things. It's a transformation, not an end. Of course, I didn't *want* to die -- or transition, for that matter. But, as I would learn later, some others who were caught in the wreckage did.

Another important teaching that I learned from The Rosicrucian Order is that the mind is divided into the objective mind, the subjective mind, and the subconscious mind. The objective mind is analytical in nature, the subjective mind controls the emotions, and the subconscious mind stores all information and memories coming from the objective and subjective mind. Now, when you request information from yourself, for example: "What's her name again?" the subconscious mind sends the answer to either the objective or the subjective mind, based on the nature of the information.

In my case, I was in big trouble. I didn't want to die, but I had no choice other than acceptance of my fate. However, due to the fact that I was asking myself, "How do I get out of this mess?" the subconscious mind was actively sending all kinds of information to my objective and subjective minds from my past experience and knowledge, hoping that something would help.

This lesson was extremely important; for I had to stay quiet, processing all information coming from my subconscious mind, analyzing it carefully and selecting the pieces I felt would be useful. It was a period where my subconscious mind, which is designed to protect me from death at any cost, was sending all kinds of information to my objective and subjective minds for consideration, in order to increase my chances of survival.

Then, I heard the voice say, "Look at your watch." My watch? Why would Jesus tell me to look at my watch? Oh my God, yes. I still had a watch. It was given to me by a wonderful friend,

THE MIRACLE OF MUSIC

Sabina Strong, as a Christmas gift in December 2008. I pressed the round little button and saw my little tomb flooded with a beautiful green light. The watch read 8:10 p.m.

I couldn't believe it. Had I really been buried for almost three hours and awake for – what? – less than one? I became really excited because I now could tell time. Well! After all, maybe, just maybe, my life was not over.

I'm very claustrophobic, which, in the dark, I'd suppressed. Now, in the light, I saw that I had some space overhead and to the right. I carefully twisted myself to lie on my side, and I could tell that there was a thick block of cement above me, Later I would find out that it was the fourth floor balcony above which had fallen on three big blocks: one in front of my head, one near my stomach, one under my right foot, and on another section of the wall itself. The blocks that caged my foot had also saved it from being crushed. Everyone has their miracles, and this was mine.

I asked Jesus, "How long I will be here?" No answer. I said, "It's so hot. And dusty. Could you please make this place cooler?" Amazingly, a breeze swept through just then. I felt hopeful for the first time. I found out later that the breeze came as a result of some big blocks of rubble that my driver and Veriole, a friend of Onickel, had removed just as I asked God to give me air. I found two smooth stones that became my pillow.

Then I heard voices. These weren't in my head, but above me and somewhere close. I screamed, "Can anyone hear me? Can anyone hear me ! I am alive! Can you hear me?"

Onickel answered, "Yes, we can hear you, and we will do everything possible to get you out. We are not leaving you behind. Are you hurt?"

I explained my situation as best I could. I knew Onickel

would keep his word if he could. He is amazingly conscientious and level-headed. What I didn't know then was that Onickel and his four friends were also under cement blocks, but not so many, and they were able to escape very early on without much physical damage.

I kept talking, babbling in Creole. If you don't talk, you're dead. No one is going to give you the time of day, not even your best friends, if they don't know where you are, and if you're still alive.

"Oh my God," I yelled. "You guys are okay?"

"I guess," Onickel said.

"You guys are alive?"

"Yes."

"Did you get hurt?"

"No, we're okay."

Then I asked, "How is Myslie?"

"Myslie is okay."

"If I die, tell her I love her," I said.

A female voice a bit in the distance, which belonged to a friend of Onickel's, said, "I love you, too."

From where I was, it sounded like Myslie; at least I thought it was Myslie then. Now, I was at peace. Okay, my friends and Myslie were fine. I didn't have to worry about their safety any- more. However, getting me out was not going to be easy. Onickel and Siméon were totally blind. So they wouldn't be able to help clear out the debris, especially with the aftershocks, which were quite frequent. The two other people were women. One was crippled, and I don't know the condition of the other one. But I was pretty sure that these women were not going to remove the rubble. Thus, only Veriole would have tried to help.

I told myself that it was going to be a long and challenging night to stay alive. However, I had air and space. I didn't feel dizzy from blood loss – a good sign – but I was in pain. So once again I turned to Jesus. "Could you please stop the pain in my right foot?"

At once the pain lessened. And the voice told me, "Do not move the foot from where it is." I thanked Jesus for his great mercy.

Now all I had to do was stay awake and wait for help. I had lots of time to kill. Subsequently, I found out that the whole secret is to understand in such a situation is that time is your absolute best friend. Not only do you need to buy time, you also have to do your very best to remain in good physical, emotional, and mental condition. At St. Vincent's School for the Handicapped, the head nun, Sister Joan Margaret, had made it part of her mission to teach us how to deal with time. She believed that hard work and self-discipline were the keys to success. I could never let her catch me sitting around, taking a break. If she found me, she would say, "What are you doing? Why aren't you working? Don't sit there and let time go by. You have to be time-conscious."

But my watch? Why would Jesus tell me to look at my watch? What was its significance? My watch would help me keep track of time, and maybe I could use time management to deal with my pain.

At that moment, the song "My Favorite Things," from *The Sound of Music* popped into my head.

> "When the dog bites
> when the bee stings
> when I'm feeling sad

I simply remember my favorite things
and then I don't feel so bad!"

In 1999, a great friend of mine, Marjory Brook, who was a teacher in Clovernook Center for the Blind, where I was taking mobility training and home management, gave me the soundtrack as a gift, and it had made a lasting impact upon me. Three songs stood out – the first was "Climb EV'ry Mountain." Do whatever you do to find your dream. Just go. I couldn't find a better song than that. The second was "I Have Confidence." I used to listen to that song every morning before I went to class, just like I used to listen daily to a Jascha Heifetz recording before practicing the violin. Heifetz is known to be the greatest violinist of the 20th century. I always feel inspired listening to his performances. There is HEIFETZ, and there is everyone else. The third was "My Favorite Things."

"When the dog bites
when the bee stings
when I'm feeling sad
I simply remember my favorite things
and then I don't feel so bad!"

So, whenever something bad happens to you, look for your favorite things. I played those songs every day. The rest of the album was nice, but these were my lesson songs, my life songs. I began to sense a connection. Okay, so what's my favorite thing? The violin.

As a former member of the Rosicrucian order, (AMORC), I had learned about the power of visualization. Maybe it could help distract me from my situation. And that was when I made another connection and got the idea to imagine myself playing my favorite violin sonatas and concertos. I'd pick the pieces I loved the most and made me the happiest in the moments when I was performing them. I would also program each hour. I made a schedule in three parts. First I would pray. Then I would make sure my friends knew I was still alive. (They were afraid to talk to me too much. They thought I would lose energy. "Save your energy," they said. "No. If I don't talk to you I'm going to fall asleep.") And then I would play a concerto or sonata in my head. I also made some time to reflect on my life and the people I knew, and what God's purpose had been in putting me under the ground. After all, regardless of whether Jesus were present or not, I felt that he was, and for the first time in my life I could speak directly to him. So why not take advantage of it?

I think the whole key to survival when in a highly stressful situation is strategy. Think of what you have available to you in your mind and around you, and how to use it. You don't always have to prepare. I didn't prepare for the earthquake. How could I? If anything, the preparation is in your regular life. You use whatever tool is available based on your situation. *The Sound of Music* came out of nowhere and into my head. Oh yeah, I could use that. The violin was a tool. I could use that. And I didn't want to fall asleep.

I believed with all my heart that using my tools and creating a schedule of prayer, talking to my friends, and playing music in my head would help me get through the long night ahead, and whatever was still to come. The solution was visualization. I would visualize myself playing my favorite violin concertos or sonatas. I'd pick pieces I liked and program each hour. I made a schedule in three parts. I prayed and meditated for ten to fifteen minutes. I made sure my friends knew I was still alive by speaking to them for five to ten minutes, and performed a concerto or other favorite violin work for thirty to forty-five minutes, in my head.

I had learned about visualization when I'd studied with the Rosicrucian Order. Visualization doesn't mean just seeing something in your head. True visualization, the kind I'm speaking about, is a mystical experience. It's trance-like. An obvious question would be, "But if you're playing something sad, aren't you wrenched back to reality because it reminds you of how sad you are to be buried alive?"

No. True visualization means I am *not* in the hole. I'm not in the earthquake space. I am somewhere else, doing something else. Even in the best of circumstances you need to be very focused, and in my situation I needed to virtually transport myself to another place and time. The fear of being in the hole, the pain in my feet, the fear of how long I might be buried – all that would be too distracting to simply recall notes in my head. I had to disappear into the entire experience. And so, I prepared myself to visualize the first piece:

Mozart's Sinfonia Concertante for Violin, Viola, and Orchestra K. 364, from 9:00 to 10:00 p.m. With my daughter, Victoria, on the viola, we'd performed the Concertante in 2006 with the Holy Trinity School Orchestra, in their music hall, which was completely destroyed by the earthquake.

Mozart composed the Sinfonia Concertante in the summer of 1779, while touring Europe. He was twenty-three years old. A concertante is technically a cross between a symphony and a concerto. It brings together elements of the Baroque concerto grosso and the classical sonata, with memorable orchestral themes, sensitive melodies for the soloists, and a magnificent interplay between the two. This is one of my favorite compositions not only because Mozart wrote some of the most beautiful and flawless melodies in the classical music repertoire, but because of the excitement I find in the dialogues between the violin and the viola. It's a friendly competition and an intelligent conversation between two great players whose parts are equally difficult.

When the visualization begins, I'm in the hole. Then I'm not. I am in my car. I see Holy Trinity School out the window. Victoria and I get out of the car, taking our instruments from the back seat. Together we walk up the stairs and go to little rooms where we warm up, playing scales. Then someone walks in and says it's time to start. As we walk onstage, the audience applauds. We take our places near the conductor and wait. The stage is really hot. The breeze is too warm and I'm sweating in my suit. I smell Victoria's perfume. I hear the whoosh of the conductor's baton in the air, and the stage floor vibrates beneath my feet as the orchestra strikes the first chord.

The Sinfonia Concertante's first movement is *"allegro maestoso,"* which means played powerfully, with majesty. The work begins with a striking, long E-flat major chord followed by two semi-long and two short chords. The precision of these chords provokes an immediate emotional catharsis. What's also interesting and different from some of Mozart's other concertos is that the orchestral introduction does not introduce any of the themes played by the violin and viola soloists. In addition, the orchestral interludes throughout the first movement refer back to the introduction.

The soloists meanwhile stand center stage, in the style of a concerto grosso, instruments pointed down in the resting position, waiting patiently for their moment while the orchestra continues to introduce different melodies between the strings and winds. The contrast is dynamic, especially the E-flat pedal point in the lower strings which seems to beat like my heart.

Six measures before the introduction ends, Victoria and I look at each other, as if to say, "Our time has arrived." We bring up our instruments to playing position, making sure that we have our fingers on the right E flats since we have to play the same notes an octave apart for the first six measures of our solo. Once we start, I of course follow the rule where I have to play softer than Victoria since her notes on the viola are an octave lower than mine.

But standing there, I'm paying attention to these passing details. I am focused on one thing. At Juilliard, performers are taught to pick one thing to concentrate on as they play, and stick to it. For me, it's bow direction: making sure that my violin is held under my chin, parallel to the floor, and that my bow is parallel to the bridge. I focus to make sure the bow doesn't run onto the bridge or the fingerboard. And that's it. The rest, my analysis of a composition's moods and dynamics, my familiarity with a composer's intentions, how I feel about the emotions in the piece – all that is part of my practice and is already so ingrained that I can do it without thinking.

The first movement continues with a group of flowing, melodic dialogues between the violin and viola in which we try, in a true spirit of positive and constructive competition, to outshine each other. Then we finally arrive at the cadenza, which means the point at which the orchestra stops playing and gives the soloists the space to show off, playing in free time – meaning without a strict cadence.

THE MIRACLE OF MUSIC

I love this cadenza not only because it's technically difficult, but because it's full of tonality changes and requires extreme focus by the soloists in order to stay together. The cadenza section ends with a trill which both Victoria and I have to play together and end exactly in time, on the last note. No problem. All our practice pays off perfectly.

To our surprise, the audience breaks out in applause. According to tradition they are supposed to remain quiet – but it is great to hear their joy. Another way of understanding this movement – and the rest – is to think of the composition as a story that follows the musical line. You can even separate the instruments into voices. The better story you create, the better your performance.

Start for example by imagining that it's Christmas and your parents gave you a toy you've always wanted. The first movement is about you going through the yearly ritual of ripping open the box in anticipation, talking excitedly to your parents, and being very happy about the gift. It's a wonderful toy.

The second movement is about how you made too much noise playing with your new toy or didn't stop playing with it when you had something else to do, and your mother took it away. You cry. You see your friends playing with their toys, but not you. You long to join them. You wish you hadn't made your mother mad.

As such, this movement is very slow – *andante* – in C minor, and is one of the saddest pieces of music I've ever heard and played. It always reminds me of a funeral march, and you're crying the whole time. Sometimes, when practicing, I think of my two best friends – both blind -- who were set afire for political reasons. Other times, I think of when I received the news that my father died in December 1983. The anger, frustration, hopelessness, and resignation are immediately present.

This movement features question-and-answer phrases in which the soloists seek to surpass each other in expressing a heart-wrenching profundity of emotion. Contrary to the first movement, the orchestral introduction is short but it's related to the first melody, which I introduce. Again, a series of dialogues between the violin and viola follows, as well as orchestra interludes with key changes and alternation between major and minor keys.

Then comes the other cadenza. Instead of trying to show technical flair, Victoria and I channel the movement's utter sadness. This time the audience offers no response as the movement ends with a trill and the orchestra's funeral-like march. I guess we were able to send them into a full meditative mood.

The third movement -- an extended rondo finale, *presto,* which means in exhilarating high spirits, will jolt them awake! Happy and childlike – which reflects the fact that Mozart never really left his childhood – this rousing movement is very fast, in E-flat Major, with a semi-long orchestral introduction. I begin the solo passage and just like before, a series of dialogues between the two instruments follows. But unlike the first and second movement, the final movement has no cadenza. I get to play the last part of the final dialogue, making sure I hit those high notes just right – especially since Victoria, who played the same passage immediately before me, had hers perfect. The entire orchestra concludes the performance on a joyous high.

The audience jumps to their feet, the applause loud and enduring. We have to return to the stage several times. The orchestra presents Victoria with a bouquet of roses. I get a CD. Afterward, we leave the music hall and linger outside, where members of the audience congratulate us personally.

Here, our story concludes with your mother asking you to do something around the house. You do it well, she is pleased, and she gives back your toy. You're happy again, but in a more satisfying way than at first. Then you just wanted the toy. This time you've missed it. The reward of its return is more powerful.

Then suddenly I was back in reality, back under the ground, conscious once again of pain. I cried out to my friends to let them know I was still alive. This time, I didn't hear just Onickel and his cousin/driver Veriole, but my driver, Marcel, was there as well. I was even happier.

"Marcel!" I exclaimed. "Aren't you supposed to be home at this time?"

He said, "I got as far as Sacré Coeur Church [which is a two-minute walk from the school]when the earthquake began. So I came back here to see if everyone was okay."

He helped my friends who were trapped, and he went to different places outside to find some tools to remove me out from under the rubble as well. At this time, he was telling me about the devastation of Port-au-Prince, how the National Palace and other important buildings went down. I couldn't believe it.

Now, besides Veriole, Marcel was there removing rubble. He assured me that he would try to find Boss Sonson to help. But unfortunately, there was no phone communication. Then I went back to perform my next piece of music. I said a prayer, and selected the next concerto to get away from my little tomb.

ROMEL JOSEPH

Tchaikovsky Violin Concerto -- 10:00 p.m.- 12:20 a.m.

The Violin Concerto in D major, Op. 35, written by Pyotr Ilyich Tchaikovsky in 1878, is one of the best-known of all violin concertos. It is also considered to be an emotional work and among the most technically difficult and lyrical works for violin. It is unquestionably one of my favorite pieces in the violin repertoire. As with most concerti, the piece is in three movements:

Allegro moderato (D major)
Canzonetta: Andante (G minor)
Finale: Allegro Vivacissimo (D major)

There is no break or pause between the second and third movements. A typical performance runs approximately thirty-five minutes. The piece was written in Clarens, a Swiss resort on the shores of Lake Geneva, where Tchaikovsky had gone to recover from the depression brought on by his disastrous marriage to Antonina Miliukova.

Since 1972, when I received the LP 33 record of the life of Tchaikovsky as a Christmas gift, I had always dreamed of performing this work with the Haiti Holy Trinity Philharmonic Orchestra. This dream finally materialized in June 1994. Once again, I disappeared from my little tomb to the night of that performance. I was in the tomb -- then at once I was at Holy Trinity.

It is around 7:00 p.m., on a warm breezy evening. I walk to the black gate of Holy Trinity, all excited and happy. I first find a room, warm up quietly, and decide to sit in the audience to listen to Cynthia Racine, daughter of the orchestra conductor

THE MIRACLE OF MUSIC

Julio Racine, an excellent cellist, who starts the concert with the Camille Saint-Saens Concerto for Cello and Orchestra. Her interpretation of the concerto is superb. She receives a standing ovation following her performance, which was truly awesome.

Right after she walks off the stage, a beautiful lady of medium height sees me sitting by myself in the back of the hall. She comes to me and says: "Wow! She is extraordinary, isn't she?"

I reply, "Yes, she certainly is."

Then she says, "You are going to play after her?"

I reply, "Yes, I play during the second half."

She continues, "You certainly have a challenge; do you think the public will like your performance as much as hers?"

"I don't know. We'll see." I said, And I walk out of the hall. I go back to the room where I was warming up, take my violin, play around some, and within a few minutes, the conductor comes for me. It is my time.

The second half of the concert begins with the second movement of Beethoven's Symphony No. 7. I am anxious, waiting impatiently for the piece to end. Finally it it is over. The stage hands then move the orchestra further back on the stage to make room for me, and I walk in under a warm applause from the public. I look and smile at the audience. The hall is completely full; about 470 in attendance; after all, this is the first time the Tchaikovsky violin concerto was going to be performed live in Haiti.

We all tune our instruments, and the performance begins with a short orchestral introduction. Then, I come in with a brief cadenza followed by a beautiful melody in D major. This movement is in sonata form. In typical Tchaikovsky style, the work continues with difficult passages, which contain repetitions, sequences, and endless scale passages which lead to the beautiful lyrical second theme in A major, which I love.

The theme is followed by a very emotionally unstable passage which contains dialogues between the soloist and the orchestra and ends in a highly difficult and brilliant manner. Whoof! Here comes the orchestral tutti. I get to rest for a while. Then comes a fun and interesting passage which is a development-like section, where the soloist can really show his/her virtuosity. It's a variation on the main theme. Then comes another big orchestral tutti followed by the cadenza, which of course is truly difficult to play; especially the last eight measures.

The cadenza ends on a trill and the orchestra quietly comes in with the main theme which is the recapitulation. Tchaikovsky concludes this movement with one of the most brilliant codas imaginable. It's happy, exhilarating, festive, and euphoric. I feel like my brain is going to explode with joy. The public stands up at once and applauds for a long time.

Then we enter the second movement, which is a simple song, and can be characterized as tranquil and melancholic. It contains two magnificent melodies. The first one in G minor, and the second in E-flat major. This movement is followed by a rather long crying-like orchestral tutti, and then comes an ecstatic intro to the third movement. The violin solo enters with a humorous cadenza followed by the fast and really happy third movement, which is a rondo.

The first section is fast, with a lot of difficult passages. It makes me feel like I am running a horse race. This fast passage is followed by a section in A major which starts slowly and majestically and gradually goes faster.

Through the rest of the piece, Tchaikovsky maintains clear and distinct contrasts between fast and slow passages, as well as major and minor keys. In this movement, I have the most fun near the end where there are dialogues between the soloist and the orchestra, as well as long scale passages.

The public is elated and I am extraordinarily happy, for one of my childhood dreams has materialized. I then spend some time backstage greeting members of the audience, and I am again transferred back to my little tomb.

I look at my watch, and it is 12:20 a.m. "Wow!" I said, "That was a long time. I hope my friends think that I am still alive. They probably thought I went to sleep." So I called out for them and I talked to my driver for quite a while.

He had been my driver since January 2004, and knew me very well. He assured me that he and the others would do what they could to get me out. I told him that I was instructed that I should try everything possible in order not to fall asleep; because if I did, I might not wake up.

Then I prayed for a while, asking God that if I should live, to guide my life and to help me become a better person; and if I should die, to please protect my soul. Then I once again went back to the violin.

Franck Sonata in A Major -- 1:00 to 2:00 a.m.

I have selected this violin sonata written in 1886, because it is beyond a doubt one of my favorites. I performed it in many recitals, including my final recital at Julliard in May 1987, with Karin Schwarz, my wonderful pianist. I chose this venue as the place I would use for visualization. So from my little tomb, there I was on stage at Juilliard.

The hall was about three-quarters full with my friends, as well as other students and teachers who came for this performance. This sonata was the last work I had to play for the recital.

This is an extraordinary, ingeniously written sonata for violin and piano by César Franck. He was born in Liège, Belgium, on December 10th, 1822, and became a French citizen in 1873, where he made his home until he died on November 8th, 1890. In his compositions, he sought to incorporate the achievements of Romanticism in an essentially classical framework, with a harmonic idiom influenced to some extent by the chromaticism of Liszt and Wagner. Composed in 1886, the Violin Sonata in A Major is one of the finest examples of Franck's use of cyclic form, a technique he had adapted from his friend, Franz Liszt, in which themes from one movement are transformed and used over subsequent movements.

After a few minutes' rest from the first part of the recital, Karen and I walk back on stage. I tune my violin, and she makes sure that I am ready. She starts with a short introduction which consists of four sets of three quiet chords, for a total of twelve chords, ($1+2=3$, a prime number) which produces a feeling of uncertainty. Then I begin with the first melody, which has two groups of eight notes (a total of sixteen notes, $1+6=7$, a prime number) which is the cyclical theme to be used throughout the four movements of the work.

Although the first movement, *Allegretto ben moderato,* is in A major, it begins in B minor and progresses in a wandering tonality fashion until near the end of the piece where it maintains the key of A major. As I perform this first movement, it gives me the feeling of nobility and tranquility.

Then comes the powerful fiery second movement in D major, marked *Passionato,* which inspires in me the feelings of passion, anger and rage. It is filled with dynamic contrasts as well as constant mood changes.

THE MIRACLE OF MUSIC

The third movement, *Recitativo-Fantasia,* is the most original movement in the sonata. It starts with a quiet piano introduction. Then the violin makes its entrance with an improvisation-like passage (which is the fantasia of the title), and the entire movement is quite free in both structure and expression. Moments of whimsy alternate with passionate outbursts. This movement is full of varied emotions, beautiful melodies, and contrasting passages which I so enjoy playing.

After the expressive freedom of the third movement, the finale restores order with pristine clarity. It is a canon in octaves, which starts with the piano, followed by the violin at the interval of a measure. This first expressive lyrical melody is of rare beauty. Interestingly, it is followed by one of the themes from the third movement, first played by the piano with a violin variation, then vice versa. In the subsequent theme, Franck returns to one he introduced in the first movement, which is very sad, yet has an exciting manner. Then out of nowhere, one of the tragic themes from the third movement resurfaces and finally, the first part of the movement reappears with a beautiful, exciting, and brilliant coda. If you are not a musician, this movement can really confuse you, for Franck used many of the melodies of the previous movements in the last.

The audience is happy and we all go to a reception following the performance, where I am able to talk to my friends, teachers, and others who are present. Then, suddenly I was back to my little tomb once again. It was now 1:40 a.m. I stayed quiet for a while, praying to Jesus so that he might reveal to me my mission and purpose for the rest of my life, if I were to be rescued.

Then I called out to my friends and I found Marcel. I gave him the phone numbers to call my sister Gilberte, my youngest brother, Jean-Maret, and my great friend, Carole Léveillé, who lived one block away from me. Carole was, and still is one of my most trusted friends. I knew she would make sure that I was rescued, no matter what. She has the will, and the necessary contacts to make a difference. In fact, on January 12th, 2000, when The Victorian School was first destroyed by fire, she was most supportive and allowed Sherry, Victoria, and me to stay at her house for 6 months until I was able to have a room once again in the school. Marcel sadly informed me the phones were not working. So, I once again decided to continue my performance through visualization by selecting my next piece.

Alexander Glazunov: Concerto for Violin and Orchestra Op. 82 -- 2:00 to 3:00 a.m.

Alexander Konstantinovich Glazunov was born in St. Petersburg on August 10th, 1865, and died in Paris on March 21st, 1936. His deeply expressive violin concerto, in A minor, Op. 36, a composition steeped in the rich expressiveness of the romantic tradition, was composed between 1904 and 1905, and premiered on March 4th, 1905, in St. Petersburg, with Leopol Auer as soloist. This concerto is the most widely performed of all Glazunov compositions. It is a richly melodic work, in which the expressive and technical potential of the violin is fully realized.

"Within Russian music, Glazunov has a significant place, because he succeeded in reconciling Russianism and Europeanism," wrote Boris Schwarz. He is a synthesis of Rimsky-Korsakov's orchestral virtuosity, the lyricism of Tchaikovsky, and the contrapuntal skill of Taneyev.

THE MIRACLE OF MUSIC

This concerto elegantly wraps up various Romantic concepts, and takes on the concerto concept in an easily grasped package. The three movements of the traditional concerto are contained within the fast-slow-fast structure of this work's single movement, and the entire work unfolds from the melodic material stated at the beginning, giving the concerto the character of a single sonata-form movement.

The moody slow section serves as a development of the opening material and builds to a spectacular cadenza. The final section, serving the function of a recapitulation, unleashes more soloistic fire.

I first heard the Glazunov concerto in a master class of Dorothy Delay in March 1981, performed by a student named Jenny. I instantly fell in love with it, and decided that would be the piece I would learn in the summer of 1981, while I was at Tanglewood, Massachusetts with my new teacher, Joel Smirnoff, a member of the Boston Symphony Orchestra. I had immeasurable fun learning it, and I believe it is the most well-written concerto for the violin that I've ever heard or performed.

My visualization took me back to June 2008, when I performed this concerto at Holy Trinity in Port-au-Prince. I was especially happy that day because, since the orchestra doesn't have a harp, Bradley, my son, played the harp part on the piano, and Victoria was playing in the viola section. At that point, I mentally left my tomb to perform.

It is, of course, a very hot day. Every day is hot when you live in Haiti. But luckily, the air conditioning is working in the hall. Around 11:30 a.m., following the intermission to the first part of the concert, the orchestra conductor, David Cesar, comes to get me in his office where I am warming up. We walk on stage.

The hall is completely full. The audience applauds our entrance. I shake the concertmaster's hand, tune my violin, and we start.

The piece is in a romantic sonata form; that is, the development and recapitulation come at the end of the second slow movement, as opposed to the middle of the first movement. The work begins with a short orchestral introduction, and the violin comes in with a beautiful but sad melody in A minor. This melody is highly significant, for Glazunov built the whole melodic and harmonic structure of the work on three motifs which are derived from the original melody.

Motif one consists of seven notes, and begins on the second note of the melody: 1. (mi) 2. (fa) 3. (mi) 4. (ré sharp) 5. (do) 6. (si) and 7. (ré)

The second and third motifs also come from the melody. They are composed of six notes: ascending notes: 1. (la) 2. (do) 3.(mi) 4. and descending: (sol) 5. (fa sharp) 6. (Fa natural).

Furthermore, he divides these six notes into two independent motifs: (la do me) (sol) which is a minor seventh, F sharp, and F natural, as a descending chromatic motif. Note that (sol) is part of both motifs. These thematic ideas ingeniously unify the different sections and movements of the concerto.

The movement continues with a short variation on the melody, then comes a dialogue between the violin and the orchestra which introduces a second gorgeous theme in F major. This section, which is recognized as the second part of the exposition, ends with power and bravura.

It is followed by an orchestral tutti which I would call a confusing harmonic mess! I say this because when we get to this part, I feel like I don't know where I am emotionally. It uses motif one, and resolves into F major, and introduces the slow second movement which begins with a short cadenza on the violin, followed by the most gorgeous melody in D-flat major -- five flats! Violinists don't really like flats, but oh well!

This movement is full of mood changes, harmonic contrast, and double stops -- passages which are heavenly to play. This particular section ends quietly, with the violin solo and the harp, playing gorgeous arpeggios, supported by the orchestra.

Here, Glazunov comes back with a tutti where the orchestra is elaborating on the two principal themes of the first movement. It seems that's where the development of the sonata form is found.

Suddenly, the solo violin, out of nowhere, comes in with one of the most difficult passages in the piece. I used to spend one hour a day just practicing this passage during the ten weeks at Tanglewood. It is hard to memorize due to its wandering tonality. It is emotionally scary. Here, the descending chromatic three notes are strongly emphasized in the higher register of the violin.

The section continues with a form of quasi-recapitulation which leads to a brilliant and powerful cadenza. I always experience a scary feeling while I am playing the end of the cadenza because it makes me feel like I am having a bad dream.

However, the next section comes in as if the darkness is slowly disappearing and I am starting to see light. The orchestra comes in with a pedal point in the timpani and low-register instruments while the solo violin is showing off with tremolo double stops and brilliant arpeggio passages. Finally, the third movement begins with a celestial like melody in the trumpets, as if Jesus was ascending from heaven. Then, the violin repeats the melody in a majestic fashion. The movement continues as such with its powerful and relentless energy up to the end.

The audience at once stands and applauds for a long time. I walk on and off the stage several times. As I am on stage, I ask Bradley and Victoria to come forward and join me. It is such a glorious moment. Then I walk backstage, spending time with members of the audience, who are quite impressed with my performance.

Then once again, I was back in my little tomb. It was 2:46 a.m. I made it for almost ten hours. I was wondering how many more hours I would have to stay in this small tomb before I would be out in the world again -- if at all?

I called out for my friends out there, and I talked with them for a while; I could still hear them trying to move the rubble above me. But they didn't have the tools needed to break the hard cement. So, I once again prayed for a while, and then I selected my next piece.

Scottish Fantasy in E-flat major Op. 46. for Violin and Orchestra by Max Bruch -- 3:00 to 4:00 a.m.

This wonderful work was completed in 1880, and was dedicated to the virtuoso violinist, Pablo de Sarasate. It's a fantasy based on Scottish melodies. The "Scottish Fantasy" is one of the several signature pieces by Bruch which is still widely heard today.

I selected this piece because it has given me many hours of joy learning it and performing it. One of the reasons that I had studied it is because it's full of wonderful scales and arpeggios which I really needed at that time in 1981 to improve my left-hand technique.

THE MIRACLE OF MUSIC

The space of visualization was at the Cincinnati Conservatory of Music Recital Hall in February 1982, where I performed this work for my senior recital, with piano accompaniment. As I was in the little tomb, I disappeared onto the recital hall back stage, where I join my pianist, whose name is Mary. We have just enjoyed a few minutes' rest, after performing "Praeludium and Allegro" by Fritz Kreisler and Beethoven's "Romance in F major." Now, we are ready to walk back on stage under the audience's applause and start with the "pièce de résistance" for this recital.

The first movement, *Introduction; Grave, Adagio Cantabile*, starts with an orchestral introduction in E- flat minor, like a funeral march with the harp playing a key role. I must also mention that though I may be accompanied by a piano for a piece which is written for violin and orchestra, because I memorize the parts of the different instruments, I still hear them through the piano transcription.

The violin comes in with a lugubrious melody. As it continues, it projects a feeling of anger and emotional distress. This solo section is followed by an orchestral tutti, where the composition changes from E- flat minor to E-flat major, and the violin comes in with a nice, less tenebrous melody. I especially love to play this section because of the double stops found in the passages.

The second movement, *Scherzo; Allegro* in G major , is really a fun dance and a joy to play. It's light, with tempo changes, contrasting moods, and really technically difficult. I especially love to play the section where the flute and the solo violin have the most sumptuous dialogue.

The violin ends this section with a series of arpeggios and a trill. An orchestral tutti follows, and the violin comes in with a gloomy transitional melody in C minor which leads to the third movement: *Andante sostenuto* in A-flat major. The melody is beautiful and simple. It's the most romantic and lyrical of the four movements.

The fourth movement, *Finale; Allegro Guerriero,* is a powerful war-like march with several variations on the main theme. This movement really offers the opportunity for the soloist to show his/her virtuosity. I truly love the arpeggio passage at the end of the movement which is followed by a brief appearance of the second theme from the second movement, and finally, the superfast two octaves of the B-flat scale.

The audience is really happy and I receive a long standing ovation. Then, we all are invited to a small reception room on the first floor hosted by Sue Harper, a wonderful lady who was instrumental (no pun intended!) in helping with my musical studies. There, I have the chance to socialize with all my friends and teachers, and from there, I go back to my little tomb. It was 3:45 a.m.

At this time, I was getting really tired. I prayed to Jesus, asking him to please give me physical and mental energy to continue with my survival strategies, for him not to allow me to feel hungry or thirsty, so I wouldn't become dehydrated. Then I talked to my friends for a while. They must have been getting tired too, because there was no removal of rubble as earlier. Then, I went back once again to the next piece of music.

Jean Sibelius: Violin Concerto in D minor, Op. 47 -- 4:00 to 5:00 a.m .

The violin concerto in D minor, Op. 47, was written in 1903, and requires extraordinary technical skills from the violinist. This is the only concerto that Sibelius wrote and it is performed frequently by some of the best soloists around the world.

Much of the violin writing is purely virtuosic, but even the most showy passages alternate with the melody. This concerto is generally symphonic in scope, departing completely from the often lighter, "rhythmic" accompaniments of many other concertos. The solo violin and all sections of the orchestra have equal voice in the piece. Although the work has been described as having "broad and depressing" melodies, several brighter moments appear against what is essentially a dark melodic backdrop.

I love this concerto because it's highly romantic. My visualization takes me back to a previous venue that I had selected -- a small hall at Tanglewood in Lenox, Massachusetts, the summer home of the Boston Symphony Orchestra. I performed this piece in a master class in July 1983, directed by Marylou Speaker Churchill, who was then principal second violin of the BSO. She was a very inspiring teacher and I had a great time working with her. There I was in my little tomb, and then I was not.

It is a hot and beautiful sunny day. I walk from the bus to Tanglewood. My stroll is most enjoyable because there are many shade trees under which I have practiced my violin for the past two summers -- 1981 and 1982. Then I walk to the room. Some students, both attendants and performers, are already present.

Then Ms. Churchill arrives, and the class begins at 1:00 p.m. One student plays before me, then it is my turn. I am able to play part of the first movement, the complete second, and the first half of the third movement; since there are other performers playing after me.

For the first movement, *Allegro moderato* in D minor, in 2/2 time, I play from the cadenza to the end, which was nice because

I love the end *Allegro molto vivace* coda with all the octave passages and the excitement it contains.

The second movement, *Adagio di molto in* in B-flat major, in 4/4 time, is one of the most beautiful second movements of all violin concertos. The whole first theme which is so sad, is played on the G string of the violin. The next section, the violin solo, using double stops, is very plaintive. Then while the orchestra is playing the main melody, the solo violin has a beautiful variation. It's as romantic as it gets. The movement ends quietly and somberly.

I perform the first half of the third movement, *Allegro, ma non tanto* (not overly fast) in D major in 3/4 time. This movement is widely known among violinists for its formidable technical difficulty and is most assuredly one of the greatest concerto movements ever written for the instrument.

The orchestral introduction sounds like a galloping horse. Then the violin comes in with a powerful melody. I particularly like to play the two-octave double-stops D major scale with up-bow staccato. This first section offers a complete and brilliant display of violin gymnastics. Then comes the first tutti, where the second theme is taken up by the orchestra and is almost a waltz, and the violin takes up the same theme in variations, with arpeggios and double stops.

Another short section concluding with a run of octaves makes a bridge into a recapitulation of the first theme. The clarinet and low brass introduce the final section. A passage of harmonics in the violin precedes a sardonic group of chords and slurred double stops. A section of broken octaves leads to an incredibly heroic few lines of double stops and soaring octaves. The brief orchestral tutti comes before the violin leads things to the finish with a D major scale up, returning down in minor (then repeated). A flurry of ascending slur-separate sixteenth notes, punctuated by a resolute D from the violin and orchestra, conclude the concerto.

There is applause from the students who are present, Ms. Churchill offers some incredibly wonderful suggestions, and from the master class room, I revert to my little tomb. It was about 4:35 a.m.

I called out to my friends outside, and my driver, Marcel, gave me the good news. "I found Boss Sonson, and he is on his way with the necessary tools to get you out." Boss Sonson has been an employee of The New Victorian School since January 2000, following the first destruction of the school by fire.

I was very excited. I knew for sure that if Boss Sonson was present, I would get out. I thanked God for his blessings and I asked him the important question: "What do you want me to do once I am out?" I heard the voice giving me a three-part message:

1. Continue doing what you have been doing with your school and music.
2. Tell the world all that I have done for you.
3. Tell the world how great God is.

Then I replied, "Please, Jesus, make it possible for me to build a great music center where children and youth can learn and perform."

The voice responded, "It will be done. I will help you." I once again thanked Jesus for his blessings and went on to the next violin piece.

ROMEL JOSEPH

Felix Mendelssohn: Violin Concerto in E minor, Op. 64. 5:00 to 6:00 a.m.

Felix Mendelssohn's violin concerto in E minor, Op. 64, was his last large orchestral work. It forms an important part of the violin repertoire and is one of the most popular and most frequently performed violin concertos of all time. It was first premiered in Leipzig on March 13th, 1845, with Ferdinand David as soloist.

The work itself was one of the first violin concertos of the Romantic era, and was influential to the compositions of many other composers. Although it consists of three movements in a standard fast–slow–fast structure and each movement follows a traditional form, the concerto was innovative and included many novel features for its time. Distinctive aspects of the work include the immediate entrance of the violin at the beginning of the first movement, and the linking of the three movements with each movement immediately following the previous one.

The concerto was initially well received and soon became regarded as one of the greatest violin concertos of all time. It remains popular and has developed a reputation as an essential work for all aspiring concert violinists to master, and usually one of the first Romantic era concertos they learn.

I learned the Mendelssohn concerto in the summer of 1976, at Tanglewood with Roger Shermont, who was then a member of the Boston Symphony Orchestra. I had lots of fun learning it, and I practiced it regularly until December 1977, when I performed it on the violin at the Haitian American Institute with the late Doctor Férerre Laguerre on the piano.

Following the 1976 Tanglewood Festival, I went back to my

home in Haiti in Carrefour, which is one of the suburbs of Port-au-Prince, practicing the concerto every day. To my amazement, many girls would come in front of my house, standing and listening. That made me very happy. They were in love with the concerto and my playing. As I was in my little tomb, I disappeared through visualization to one of my most memorable moments with this great concerto.

It is a morning in April 1977, and I have a rehearsal with the Holy Trinity Philharmonic Youth Orchestra at 9:30 a.m. As is my custom, I walk out of the boys' dorm of St. Vincent 's school, which is located behind the biggest penitentiary of Haiti, at 8:45 a.m. so I could arrive early.

From the dorm, which is on Rue l'Enterrement, I walk to Rue des Casernes, turn on Rue de la Reunion. Toward the middle of the block, I see my friend, Raymond Démangues, a sound engineer with whom I talk for a minute, then I turn on Rue Pave. As I move near "Boîte à Musique Raoul Denis," where my Tchaikovsky LP 33 came from in December 1972, I hear the introduction to the Mendelssohn violin concerto from the two speakers he has outside the store. Then comes the violin solo. I walked rapidly toward the speakers, performing the concerto, using an imaginary violin and bow. I completely forgot that I was on the street. I was just playing along with the album.

The first movement of the concerto is in E minor, in sonata form. Instead of introducing the movement with an orchestral introduction, Mendelssohn begins the work with a super-short accompaniment with an almost immediate entry of the solo violin, and a beautiful melody in E minor which is so sad, it makes me cry. The opening theme is then restated by the orchestra. The violin then comes in a frenetic chromatic transition passage as the music subsides and modulates into a tranquil second subject theme in G Major. The melody is played by the woodwinds while the violin is holding the open G string.

This beautiful, yet lugubrious tune is played by the solo violin itself before a short codetta ends the exposition section of the opening movement. The opening two themes are then combined in the development section, where the music builds up to the innovative cadenza, which Mendelssohn wrote out in full rather than allowing the soloist to improvise. The cadenza builds up speed through rhythmic shifts from quavers to quaver-triplets and finally to semiquavers, which require ricochet bowing from the soloist.

This serves as a link to the recapitulation where the opening melody is played by the orchestra, accompanied by the continuing ricochet arpeggios by the soloist. During the recapitulation, the opening themes are repeated, with the second theme being played in E major before returning to E minor for the closing of the movement. The music gathers speed into the coda, which is marked *presto*, before a variant of the original chromatic transition passage in the orchestral tutti ends the first movement.

As the orchestra ends with the movement, unusually enough, the bassoon sustains its B from the final chord of the first movement before moving up a semitone to middle C. This serves as a key change from the E minor opening movement into the lyrical C major slow movement.

The movement is in ternary form and is reminiscent of Mendelssohn's own "Songs without Words." The theme to the darker middle section in A minor is first introduced by the orchestra before the violin takes up both the melody and the accompaniment simultaneously, using double stops. The tremulous accompaniment requires nimble dexterity from the soloist before the music returns to the main lyrical C major theme, this time leading toward a serene conclusion.

The third movement, *Allegro molto vivace,* is in sonata rondo form. Following the second movement, there is a brief fourteen-bar transitional passage which has an uncertain tonality and ends with a B major chord in E minor for solo violin and strings only. This leads into the lively and effervescent finale, the whole of which is in E major and whose opening is marked by a trumpet fanfare, and requires fast passagework from the soloist.

The opening exposition leads into a brief second B major theme which is played by the soloist and builds to a series of rapidly ascending and descending scales and arpeggios, reminiscent of the cadenza from the first movement. The orchestra then plays a variation of the opening melody, before the music moves into a short development section in G major. I always anticipate the end of the development where the violin has so many notes in one up bow staccato which leads to the recapitulation.

The recapitulation is essentially similar to the exposition, apart from the addition of a counter-melody in the strings. There is almost a small cadenza near the end of the movement when the woodwinds play the main tune against prolonged trills from the solo violin. The concerto then concludes with a frenetic and euphoric coda which makes me feel victorious.

Following the third movement, a tall man walks towards me, holding an LP 33 record, and says: "Congratulations! You are going to be a great violinist some day. Here, I give you this as my gift to you. You can now listen to it at home."

Shocked and amazed, I simply say, "Thank you! Thank

you! Thank you.!" It is the album I was listening to, with Zino Francescatti as soloist.

I am elated. I continue my way to St. Trinity with my album, telling everyone what has happened. Then I returned to my little tomb. It was 5:50 a.m. I called up to my friends, who were really quiet.

"Are you people still around?"

Boss Sonson replied, " Mr. Joseph, I am here."

"Great! Great!" I said. "How are you, Boss Sonson?"

Boss Sonson said, "I am fine."

"The earthquake didn't hurt you?" I asked.

"No, thank God. I am fine and I am here to get you out."

I said, "Thank you for coming."

He replied, "Okay. I am going to start working."

I was really happy. I prayed once again, thanking God and Jesus for sending Boss Sonson and his men to save me from being buried alive, for giving me energy to perform all these classical violin pieces in my head throughout the night, and especially for the presence of Jesus in my little tomb. I further asked Jesus to renew my energy so that I could be alert, in order to help in my rescue.

8

My Rescue. Intensive Care: Airlift to America, Two Months in a Miami Hospital, Discovered by the World

On January 12th, 2010, at about 5:50 p.m., the horrible earthquake shook virtually the whole city of Port-au-Prince. Some areas -- such as Pétionville, Tabarre, and La Plaine -- were hardly affected. However, Carrefour, the city proper of Port-au-Prince, Nazon, Delmas, Bourdon, and Canapé Vèrt, were severely affected. Most of the schools and churches were destroyed. And here I was, on January 13th, around 6:00 a.m., under my little tomb, waiting to be rescued.

As I was lying there, a dialogue between Boss Sonson and me began.

Boss Sonson said, "We are going to start breaking the rubble so we can get you out. However, we need to first locate where you are. The problem is that when you speak, your voice reverberates under the whole building and all the rubble. Consequently, we cannot tell exactly where you are and that will slow down the possibility of finding you in time."

I replied, "Okay. Let's figure out where I am. The building is facing north. I am lying on the railing of the third floor. Under the railing are branches of trees which were planted in front of my room. Under the branches is the yard -- I can feel its texture with my right hand."

Boss Sonson said, "Okay."

I said, "My head is facing the street -- that means west. To my left, I can feel the dirt where the plants were."

Boss Sonson replied, "Okay. This description gives me an idea of where you are. But the line where the trees were planted goes along the whole building from east to west, and it will still take a long time to break all that cement."

I said, "Okay. Give me a minute to think about it. "

Boss Sonson said, "Okay."

Then I asked myself the question: *How do I pinpoint to him exactly where I am?* I stayed quiet for a few seconds, and the idea came to me: "Use your ears to direct him!" Here again, my musical training would save me. Because I learn all my music by ear, I am able to listen to details. For example: when I listen to a symphony orchestra, I can hear each instrument separately and am able to tell due to my perfect pitch and attention to detail, what each instrument is playing. Hence, I don't just memorize my part, but those of the other instruments. So, the solution was for me to help them find me using my ears. Then I went back to Boss Sonson.

"Boss Sonson," I said.

"Yes, Mr. Joseph?"

"I have an idea. You are going to start hitting the cement beginning near the inverter room, which is southeast of the building. You will move toward the main office and the little store. That's going west. Once you are above me, I will let you know."

Boss Sonsons said, "Okay. No problem." So he started hitting the cement. After a little while, he asked, "Can you hear me?"

"Yes," I said. "Keep moving." As he continued to hit the cement, I could hear him getting closer to me. And finally I yelled, "Okay. You are above me."

"Are you sure?" he asked.

"I believe you are," I said.

He said, "Okay. I am going to start breaking the cement. First, I will make a small hole, big enough for me to go down. And if I find you, I will enlarge it so that you can be removed."

"Sounds like a great plan," I said. "Go for it."

He said, "Okay." Then they started. While they worked, I was talking to him and my driver, Marcel, reminiscing about old times. Then suddenly, a bunch of dirt came down in front of me.

I yelled, "Stop. Boss Sonson, stop! There is dirt falling in front of my face, and that will block the air that I am breathing. You need to find a way not to let the dirt fall."

Boss Sonson said, "Okay. I know exactly where you are." He continued working with the other workers for a while, as we kept on talking about past events, such as the amazing ceramic work we did to build the stage for the children to present musical programs, the 2008 incredibly fun Christmas party we had in the school with the most amazing Christmas lighting with over 5000 Christmas lights and other decorations, etc.

As we were talking, I heard some other voices. There were Mrs. Hasboun, one of the teachers, and Ms. Damus, one of the administrative assistants. Around 7:50 a.m., I saw a big light.

"Wow! There is the sun," I said. "It's so beautiful and bright! I guess life is back again."

Boss Sonson said, "Okay. I am going to come down to you." He came down and I saw his feet.

"Hi!" I said.

Boss Sonson said, "Wow! You are really locked up. It's going to take a while to get you out."

"I guess only your hand can get to me," I said. "Do whatever you can. Could I have some water, please?"

"Okay. Wait." He said. At once he went back upstairs and in a few minutes, he came down with four big bottles of very cold water.

"Thank you," I said.

Boss Sonson said, "You are welcome. I am going back to work."

"Okay," I replied.

I took my time to slowly drink the water, one bottle at a time, which felt so good inside. As they worked, I kept on talking to Boss Sonson, and Marcel, my driver, to pass the time as they tried to get me out. Then out of nowhere, the idea came to me to find a photographer to take my picture when I am coming out of my little tomb. I wasn't sure why I needed one, but I wasn't prepared to ask questions. So I called Ms. Damus and asked her to send one of the employees to find someone on the street with a camera so that he/she could take a picture of me as I was getting out of the little tomb. I didn't know why I needed a picture of myself until two weeks later when I started to have media interviews.

Next thing I knew, a photographer came, took some pictures, and left. He didn't wait for me to get out. I never heard back from him again to see about getting copies of those pictures. Around

10:15 a.m., the workers had removed enough rubble to expose the deep hole I was in so they could finally get me out. But first, they had to break the thick cement that crushed my right foot. This was a very difficult task. Though they did their best, my foot was not only crushed, but there was a very deep laceration that split across from my ankle bone to the base of my big toe. But oh well! That was a small price to pay to stay alive.

As soon as my right foot was free, I heard the voice which had been communicating with me through the night saying, "Okay. I am leaving you now. You will be fine. Always remember this experience and what God has done for you."

I replied, "Thank you, Jesus, for everything." At once, I sensed an emptiness in the little tomb, and the pain began to get worse and worse.

I said, "Boss Sonson, both of my feet are really hurting. I need to get to a hospital."

Boss Sonson said, "We have to pull you out backwards by your feet, because it will be too dangerous to break the cement above your head. But first, we still have to cut some heavy iron before you can get out."

"Okay," I said. The pain was becoming more excruciating. I started to cry and scream. "Please hurry up. The pain will cause my blood pressure to go up."

Boss Sonson said, "How come you were so pleasant earlier?"

"Because the blood wasn't circulating in the right foot. Now it is, it's causing the pain. Please hurry up."

Finally, the big irons were removed, and I was dragged out of the tomb by my legs, and carried by a group of men. They put me on the ground, and they found one of the doors from the school building on which they put me. This door would become my bed for forty-eight hours. As both of my feet were bleeding, especially the right one, They took the shirt I had on, and wrapped my feet.

Then, they stopped a camionette -- which is like a covered pickup truck -- on the street. The workers put me on the truck to find a hospital. Some of the people who were in the school came along with me, including Benjamin, a former employee of the school who is Boss Sonson's father; Marcel, my driver; Veriole, Onickel's cousin; Ms. Damus, my administrative assistant; Mrs. Hasboun, a teacher from the English section of the school; and my wife's two brothers Colossian and Joe, whom I met for the first time.

Then I asked, "Where is Myslie?"

One young man answered, "Myslie is with her sister, Josette. Her head was slightly injured, and Josette is taking care of her. "

I asked, "Who are you?"

The young man answered, "I am Colossian." He pointed to another man sitting across from him on the truck. "And he is Joe. We are Myslie's brothers."

"That's strange!" I replied somewhat confused. "Myslie never told me that she had brothers. How come I never knew you? She told me that she only had two sisters-- namely Josette and Emilie."

Colossian said, "Well, I don't know, but we are her brothers."

Myslie was extremely secretive about her family. She always told me that her true family was her little sister, Josette, and her mother. She hated Emilie, her older sister, and told me to stay away from her. This hatred was to some extent justified.

Myslie used to live with Emilie when we were dating back in June 2008. Then around November 2008, Myslie informed me that Emilie did not approve of our relationship. She explained that Emilie was a very jealous woman who hated to see her happy. So I went on the following Sunday to Emilie's house, where Myslie had prepared a special brunch for us. I was able to talk to Emilie, letting her know that I was serious about dating Myslie, and she didn't have to worry. Emilie agreed, and I left.

But Emilie wasn't sincere. She made Myslie's life even more miserable. And finally she kicked Myslie out of her house in May 2009, and that was when she came to live with me in the school. Myslie did spent lots of time at her cousin's house; I know her as Mrs. Gady. Mrs. Gady is a wonderful woman who was severely hurt during the earth quake when a big wall of her house broke her back. She then went to the Dominican Republic for treatment where she still resides.

I also learned later that the reason that Myslie never told me about these two brothers is that she was forced by her mother and the rest of the family to be financially responsible for them, and she didn't want me to know so that I would not be scared, thinking that her family would depend exclusively on me. In addition, I learned that Myslie made all financial transactions with her brothers through her cosmetology school.

Frequently, while I was in the bathroom, the phone would ring, and I would hear her shouting, "I gave all the money that I had and I don't have any more. How much more do I have to give?" She was always under pressure from her family to find them money, and this did start to become a source of trouble between her and me.

Back to the dialogue with Colossian; "Strange! How is Myslie?" I asked.

Colossian said, "Myslie is hurt a little, but she will be fine."

I insisted, "Are you sure you are not lying to me? Because if she is still under there, I can go back, and ask Boss Sonson to help find her. She is not too far -- she is on her bed, next to the back wall of the building, under my air conditioning. That way if she is hurt, but still alive, especially since she is pregnant, we can be together. We can travel to the States for medical assistance."

Colossian said, "Yes, I am telling the truth. She is okay." Everyone was quiet during this whole conversation.

I said, "Okay. I hope to see her soon. I will wait for her in order for us to go to the States together for treatment."

This deceiving decision, not to tell me that Myslie was not yet found, apparently was approved by everyone around in order to somehow protect me. Colossian, two months later, explained that he lied to protect me. But I am still sad, and I totally regret their decision; they were making life decisions for me while I was still lucid. They didn't understand that if I wasn't of sound mind, I wouldn't have been able to help them find me, and somehow, I still can't forgive all those who prevented me from going to look for Myslie. I still cry whenever I think about that fatal moment when they all lied to me. She could have been alive downstairs, suffering, hoping somehow that I would come and save her. Even worse, I thought, especially during my sixty days in the hospital -- what if she wasn't hurt, and was still in her dark room? There was enough food and water to have kept her alive for quite a while. But no one came for her. She would probably accuse me of being a traitor for never showing up and would finally have died once she ran out of food and water. This thought made my life hell in the hospital.

I know what it felt like as I was under the rubble, and I called, "Can anybody hear me?" When I didn't hear anyone, I told myself, "Well, I guess they gave up on me." I am sure Myslie must have felt the same way.

But all of them took that option to take her away from me as if she didn't matter -- even members of her family.

We drove, looking for a hospital. But none was to be found. The roads were covered with dead bodies. Dogs were everywhere eating them. The streets smelled horrible. In addition, I was having trouble with flies that were all over me because I had blood on me. The traffic was impossible. So finally we decided to go back near the school, where we found a doctor who was giving first aid. His name is Leslie Paul-Pierre. He is an orthopedist who was treating those who had extensive problems with their legs and feet. There, they unloaded me from the truck. It was around 12:45 p.m. The pain, in the meantime, had worsened. In a few minutes, the doctor came to me.

"Hi, my name is Doctor Pierre," he said. "What happened to you?" I explained to him my situation. He then stitched my right foot, and did some kind of ajustments with the left one. Then he said, "This is a temporary solution. You need to go to a hospital as soon as possible." The pain did stop and I was temporarily okay.

Ms. Damus and Mrs. Hasboun brought some lunch -- chicken and plantains, juice and water. It was a true blessing to eat something. Then I waited for a while. As I was waiting, a young girl came. She was in immeasurable pain. She kept on saying, "Please, God, Have mercy upon me. Please lessen the pain." I could hear myself in her as she suffered immensely.

The doctor was busy with some patients -- plus, there were other patients before her. Since she was near me, I asked her, "Where were you?"

The girl said, "I was at school, and a wall fell on my foot. But Jesus was with me during the whole time and protected me from death. How about you?"

I told her that the same thing happened to me. "I was hurt in my school." Then I gave her some of my Flanax which Ms. Damus purchased for me while driving around the streets.

I said, "Here. Take these two Flanax. They will help your pain."

She took them right away and after a few minutes, she felt a little better. Later I learned that all her family died in her house, and she was the only surviver. I still wonder what happened to this girl. I hope she was as lucky as I am and lived.

Around 4:30 p.m., Onickel and Veriole came back with a camionette, which is a truck that is open in the back with benches on both sides, and two front seats. Veriole was the driver, Onickel was sitting in front next to Veriole, and I was lying on the floor in the back. Marifrance, a teacher; Olga, one of my maids; Marcel, my driver; and Bazlais, one of school security men were with me. We first tried to go to Carrefour to my sister's house so I could stay there. But the road was blocked. Too many dead bodies.

There we met with a woman who was one of the parents of a New Victorian School student. She gave me a t-shirt and a pair of shorts to wear, which was very nice of her. At least I had some clean clothes. Then, we decided to go back to the school and spend the night there on the street. I also borrowed $100 US from Onickel to buy some basic things. By then, it was around 6:30 p.m. As we were there talking, around 8:00 p.m, some police officers were screaming: "Everyone must run. There is a tsunami coming due to the earthquake."

Everyone started running everywhere and nowhere at the same time. It was pandemonium. Veriole decided, just like the other people, to run north, where he believed that we would not be affected. To make matters worse, he had little gas in the car.

I tried to tell him that if really there were a tsunami, it would have already arrived because the ocean is near us. But my words, especially in my condition, didn't matter. He finally arrived at a gas station. But we were not able to find any gas until the next day. Consequently, we spent the night in the truck at the gas station.

In the morning, Thursday January 14th, once we had gas, we went to a hospital near the area where we were. There was no room inside. A doctor came, and put an IV in my left arm, which he said would stop the swelling. But of course, it didn't. From the hospital, we went to the airport to see if planes were flying, which would have made it possible for Onickel to fly back to the states. But the people at the airport said there were no flights. So we went to The New Victorian School.

There, around 1:00p.m. I started asking for Myslie. I wanted to go to her house to see if she was there. But I was met with all kinds of arguments by everyone, advising me not to try to find Myslie. At this point, I was becoming more and more suspicious. So Veriole pretended that he went to her house. He walked around the streets somewhere, and came back saying that the family went to the provinces. I then concluded that I was going to sleep in front of the school until early Friday morning, when I would start looking for Myslie.

Onickel made a compromise with me, by proposing that we go to Pernier, a safer area of Port-au-Prince where he had some friends. There, we would spend the night. We would come very early Friday morning to look for Myslie, to which I agreed. However, I know that looking for Myslie would have been impossible without Boss Sonson.

We went to Pernier to Onickel's friends' home, By this time, I started to feel really weak; my body was getting more and more swollen, and I started to go in and out of conciousness. Though I kept drinking water, I was getting continuously dehydrated. Onickel also purchased a wheelchair from someone for $50 US, which allowed me to get around.

Around 10:30 p.m., I was able to make a call to Miami. I left a message for my ex-wife Sherry, telling her that I was hurt but alive. But Myslie didn't make it yet. I was in total denial about her death. I didn't want to believe for a second that she died.

In a few minutes, Onickel asked me to talk to someone. It was Marie Lourdes, a person I had not spoken to or seen for at least thirty-five years. I talked to her for a while, and she was able to convince me that I should come to the States for treatment.

She was so convincing that I made the decision not to look for Myslie, and instead travel to the States the next day.

Early in the morning, we woke up. We all went to the airport. It was chaos. People were everywhere. I finally made it to the tarmac where you would board the plane. There were many US Marines giving first aid treatment to US citizens. I went to them -- they looked at my left hand and feet, and suggested that I go right away to the American Embassy for immediate entry to the States to a hospital. Veriole and Marcel took me to the American Embassy. I went through the main gate with no problem. But when I arrived in front of the main door to enter the embassy, I was greeted by a highly angry and hostile American officer.

He said, "What do you want? Why are you here?"

I replied, "I was hurt in the earthquake and my school fell on top of me. There is no room in any of the hospitals in Port-au-Prince, and according to the Marines at the airport, I must receive immediate treatment if I am to live."

The officer said, "We are only taking US citizens to the States. Are you a US citizen?"

I said, "Yes, since April 2005."

He continued, "Do you have proof of citizenship? Do you have an American passport with you?"

"I do have one, but it's underground in a carry-on suitcase, near my bed, next to my dead wife," I said.

The US Officer persisted, "How do I know then that you are not just a regular Haitian on the streets? We have no room here in the embassy to save Haitians."

"Just like all Americans, I have a social security number which can be entered into the computer," I said.

He said, "Okay. Give me your social security number, and if

we don't find you in the system, I will throw you out back on the streets."

I said, "For real?"

He replied, "You bet I will."

"Though you can tell that I am now both crippled and blind. Would you really do that?" I asked.

"You bet! I would," he said.

"How humanitarian of you!" I observed.

He looked at me for a second or two. I could feel the rage in him. He then went inside, and in a few minutes he came back.

The officer said, "Okay, go in." Veriole started to push my wheelchair towards the door. The officer started screaming. "NOT YOU!" He pointed to Veriole. "You CAN'T go with him."

"Ok. So how do you expect me to go in? as you can see, my left hand is broken," I said.

He then went inside and came out with a woman to push me inside. I said goodbye to Veriole. Once I was inside, they took me to a clinic, looked over my wounds, and a doctor said, "He has to go now. His case is critical."

They gave me a paper which I had to give to immigration. Then the officer asked me, "Is there anyone that you would like accompany you and assist you in the hospital?" My answer was no, because to look for someone would have delayed my departure. Now, I regret that decision. I know that one must never reside in a hospital for any length of time without someone with you. The embassy workers put me on a stretcher.

Then I asked,"How about my wheelchair?"

"I think you should forget about it," said the officer. Then they walked me into a helicopter, which took me to the airport; I was transferred to a military plane and I went to Miami.

While I was on the plane, I was asked, "Which hospital would you like to go to?"

My answer was Jackson Memorial Hospital. I knew at Jackson I would have a greater chance of survival. From the military airplane, I was transfered to a helicopter which took me to the Ryder Trauma Center.

They called my daughter, Victoria, and my son, Bradley, who came instantly. Because I was going in and out of conciousness, I don't really remember what happened from the time I arrived in the hospital until I woke up hours later. I vaguely remember the doctors asking me all kinds of questions.

One doctor asked, "How did you hurt your eye?"

I replied, "What's wrong with you? Can't you see that I have no left eye?"

I also remember insisting that I wanted water. But the doctors refused. "No. sorry. We cannot give you water."

I said, "God saved me from the earthquake, and now you doctors are out to kill me by not giving me water. I spent four days with almost no water! You won't even let me wet my mouth!!" What I didn't know is that you cannot have water twelve hours before surgery.

Then, the doctor said, "We need to go now."

I said, "No, not yet. I want to see my kids. I almost didn't see them ever again! I might not wake up from surgery and I want to spend time with them." The doctor said, "Okay."

He gave me two minutes. I talked to them for a while, though I don't remember the contents of the conversation. I told them goodbye, then I have only a vague memory of what happened next.

Below, I want to share the written thoughts of my daughter,

Victoria; my ex-wife, Sherry, and one of my very best friends, Cecilia, covering the period from January 12th to the time of my arrival to Miami and my admission to the hospital.

Victoria Joseph

On January 12th, 2010, I remember waking up very late that day because I was absolutely exhausted from the weekend prior. I had just returned from my first Caribbean cruise with some of my close friends. That day was just like any other day -- had lunch with my boyfriend, Jose, whom I live with. Most of the conversation was on the topic of the recent disagreements I had been having with my father about the problems I was contributing to in his organization, Walenstein Musical Organization. Mostly my lack of focus, communication, and efficiency in accomplishing important tasks due to a lot of personal problems I was having, which affected my work.

Naturally, my father was concerned on a personal level, as well, but as he always says, "No one is going to care why you're not getting stuff done because at the end of the day, it needs to be done!" The night before, he called me to ask how my cruise was and asked if I would be able to work on the important and overdue assignments I was behind on. I told him "yes" and he continued to lecture me as to how important they were and why they needed to be done. "If you can't do it, just say so and I'll have someone else do it, but don't tell me you're going to do it and not do it!" I knew he was right and had every reason to be frustrated.

I felt terrible since I've always had trouble not letting my personal life affect my professional life. The conversation didn't end on a good note as I really was just trying to get him to end his lecture so I could go to sleep, since I was exhausted. I never realized that this could have potentially been the last conversation I had with my father.

Anyway, I went through my usual routine. I picked up my brother, Bradley, from school at 2:30 p.m. and came back home to catch up on some much-needed household chores. As I was folding my laundry, I received a text message from a co-worker at the spa I worked at, Shavon Etan, and it read "Hey! Did you hear about the earthquake in Haiti?" I had absolutely no idea what she was talking about. Living in Miami, I was more knowledgeable about hurricanes.

I replied, "No. What earthquake? When?"

She then said, "There was a 7.0 earthquake in Haiti. It's all over the news."

As I rushed over to the TV, I told Jose what I had just learned and he immediately began to Google the Richter scale so he could inform me on how bad a 7.0 earthquake was. As he was Googling, I dialed my father's number in Haiti at 5:36 p.m. and it went straight to voicemail. Naturally, I was extremely concerned. What I saw on CNN was shocking! I couldn't believe what I was seeing. I began to call everyone I could think of! My brother, my mother, my cousins, etc. Friends of mine and my father who heard about it were calling and texting me, as well. My phone couldn't handle all the "traffic" it was getting at that point!

My brother came over my house immediately with his girlfriend, Allison. We all sat in the living room glued to CNN. Once pictures of the National Palace were discovered and how badly it was damaged, I knew the odds of our home and school being okay were slim to none since we lived walking distance from there. The possible scenarios of what could have happened to my dad were endless! Where could he possibly be at 5 p.m.? Running errands and in the streets somewhere? Or even worse, could he be in a building, such as a bank, with poor structure? Could he be in his room on the first floor, working?

Then thoughts of my stepmother came to mind, as her situation would affect my father's, as well. Were they together? I know she had regular doctor's appointments since she was seven months pregnant. Could they be at a hospital or clinic somewhere together? That would be terrible, as most of the hospitals and clinics were badly damaged.

I almost had a panic attack. Uncertainty is so cruel. The more I called father, the more worried and guilty I became. I kept saying to myself, "This can't be it! I'm not ready for this. I'm not ready for him to be gone. I don't WANT him to be gone! This isn't how things are supposed to be." I couldn't say these things out loud as I had to be the stronger older sister to Bradley. He was not only concerned about my father, but also for many of the friends he made during his two-year stay in Haiti for the beginning of his high school tenure. I kept telling him, "I'm sure Pappy is fine! Don't worry. He's probably hanging around somewhere looking for some griot [fried pork] to eat."

Griot is one of my father's favorite Haitian dishes, so much so that he always told me he wanted to be buried with a plate in his coffin. What I couldn't tell him was that I was REALLY hoping that I, myself, didn't really believe what I was saying. It just seemed like the right thing to say at the time to calm him down, the same way Jose had done for me prior to Bradley's arrival.

Hours passed by and of course, Bradley and I, still completely focused on the TV, couldn't help but sit in silence. Everyone knew we were thinking the worst, but no one could convince us otherwise. I kept thinking, "What wouldn't I do now to have twelve missed calls within five minutes as he's famous for doing with me, or another bossy e-mail as to what needs to be done?"

At that point, Allison and Jose kept pressuring us to eat. I said, "How could I eat? There are millions of people in Haiti who are starving right now! My dad could be hungry and thirsty. I'm not eating!" After much convincing, we ate dinner and went back to the TV. By then, it was nightfall in Haiti. No lights. No communication. Nothing. The news was repetitive at the point since no new information could be obtained.

Allison took Bradley home, as it was a school night. Jose changed the channel and stayed by my side as he tried to distract me by putting on a movie. During the beginning of the movie, I repeatedly checked my e-mail and responded to the many text messages I received. He then took my phone and shut it off.

"You need to take your mind of this for a little bit or else you're going to go crazy! Your dad wouldn't want that. Give your phone a break and enjoy this movie!" Of course, I fought him. Taking my phone? You must be insane! He then said, "Fine. Let's make a deal. Watch this movie in its entirety, and I'll not only give you your phone back, but put the TV back on CNN." I responded, "Fine, but don't shut my phone off! My dad might call." He agreed.

After watching the movie, as promised, Jose put it back on CNN. At that point, Wyclef was on with Anderson Cooper. It was refreshing to see how people were making an effort to go and help immediately. I stayed up most of the night and watched the news. Jose would check up on me periodically and when I finally did fall asleep, he changed the channel.

January 13th, 2010, was even harder. Couldn't sleep much the night before and the fact that I didn't know what was happening with my dad made it even worse. People kept asking me how I was doing. My answer never changed. "Still nothing. Never knew uncertainty could be so cruel." I couldn't control the massive amount of people calling and texting my phone. My friends, my dad's friends, our family, people we worked with, and anyone we crossed paths with at some point in time who had heard the news. The more people asked me, the more I panicked. It was absolutely overwhelming. Times like these, I wish I had a secretary! Jose helped a lot with controlling the "traffic." I spent most of my day texting Bradley, still glued to the TV.

Later that evening, at 7 p.m., I had a Miami Symphony Orchestra rehearsal, as I am one of the violists in that ensemble. I contemplated telling them that I couldn't go, but I didn't know the director or any of the staff on a personal level, so I was quite hesitant. I didn't want to tell them about my father because it would've been more people overwhelmed, but I had signed a contract with them and I didn't want to appear flaky and unprofessional. After much contemplating and advice from Jose and other fellow close friends who are also members of the orchestra, they all advised me to go anyway since they felt I needed a distraction from the TV.

The news that day was extremely important for me as they were beginning to assess the damage of the earthquake. More pictures of important landmarks near our home were shown, and it just keep making my heart sink deeper and deeper. I would've given anything to hear from my dad or from someone who knew what the situation was with him. Rehearsal was even worse! Many of the members knew my dad because of their affiliation with his organization in Miami, so I was bombarded in person by those who had heard the news.

I'm a very discreet person about my life and its details. I didn't want to make a scene, but everyone couldn't help it. I tried to answer their questions about what happened as best as I could. The reality of it was I knew nothing except for what was on the news. All I knew is that if I had the opportunity to go to Haiti, I would, even if it meant I had to swim there!

Out of all my musician friends, the closest to me were David Andai, a violinist; and Andres Vera, a cellist. The three of us went to high school and college at the same time, played in trios together all the time, and hung out as much as our schedule permitted us to. They were actually the ones who invited me to the cruise. I value their friendship and opinion a lot. Naturally, when David told me to inform the conductor and director, Maestro Marturet, as to what was going on and how my situation might change given the opportunity to go to Haiti, I listened, since he also knew him personally.

As hesitant as I was, I told him that I would do my best to be here as contracted, but depending on my dad's condition, I might have to cancel my contract as family was my immediate concern since I'm really all my dad has. Our family was very strange, but it was always the three of us – myself, Bradley, and my father. My mom was around, but she did the best she could, considering the rollercoaster of a relationship she had with my father. Anyway, Maestro Marturet was sympathetic and told me to do what I needed to do and they would support any decision I made. That was a weight off my shoulders! I went on playing that night even though I wasn't mentally there. It got harder as they rehearsed one of my dad's favorite waltzes by Strauss.

Holding back tears was quite a challenge. No matter how hard I tried to take my mind off it, I couldn't help but go over different scenarios in my mind as to what could've happened to my father. Again, another rough night. Didn't sleep well. Didn't want to eat. All I kept doing was calling my dad's number just to hear his voice on his voicemail, praying I'd one day hear it again in person. I've never been religious, but praying seemed to be the only thing would make me feel like I was actually doing something useful.

At 10:27 p.m., three minutes before rehearsal ended, I got a call from my mother. I ignored it since I was still in rehearsal and figured I would call her back shortly. A minute later, Bradley texted me, "Call me asap! Pappy called!!!!" I immediately got out my seat mid-note with my instrument still in hand and walked outside. Everyone in the orchestra was looking at me like I was crazy! I didn't care. I called my mother as I was walking out. She told me some even better news! My dad left her voicemail. She told me he said, "I'm alive. My feet are broken. The school is completely destroyed. Myslie didn't make it. Tell Tori to keep Walenstein going. I'm going to try my best to be in the States tomorrow."

I cried! I couldn't help BUT cry! Happy tears, sad tears, worried tears, everything! Everyone walking out of rehearsal saw me on the phone, crying, as my mom tried to calm me down. Once I hung up, David and Andres were both by my side and there to give me a much-needed hug. A LONG one at that! They're really great to me. They kind of directed "traffic" elsewhere as I wasn't really in a mood to tell the same story over and over. I just wanted to go home and share the news with Jose and MAYBE get a good night's sleep.

On January 14th, 2010, I got a call at 6:59 a.m. from my cousin, Alex, in NY. He's the son of my only aunt from my father's side, Gilberte, who was also in Haiti. He got word from her that my father was alive, but that his legs were broken. My heart skipped a beat. I was SO relieved! Alex went on to tell me that the school was completely destroyed and that my father was trapped for eighteen hours under the rubble. At that point, uncertainty was no longer cruel. Even though I had a million questions, I knew Alex wouldn't be able to answer them. But my biggest reassurance was that no matter how bad things may have been, as long as my dad could speak, I knew somehow he'd be okay!

Of course, I called Bradley and texted my mother to share the good news. Jose gave me the "I told you" speech, but I was too happy to care! I was secretly happy he was right, though. Again, my phone was bombarded by calls and text messages. This time, I happily picked up and responded with the great news. Everyone was happy to hear the news, as well. I happily went to rehearsal that night again at 7 p.m. Still worried, of course, but hurt is definitely better than dead.

On January 15th, I woke up in a better mood, looking forward to my dad's possible arrival. I didn't want to get my hopes too high, but I was still excited nonetheless. Had breakfast and hung out most of the day, still trying to keep up with the massive volume of calls and text messages on my phone. Talk about GLUED to my hand! Man…anyway, I didn't have access to my car because I lent it to Jose since his wasn't working. I had him drop me off at Bradley's house so we could hang out before rehearsal later.

At 5:03, I got a call from Jackson Memorial Hospital on Friday asking if I knew someone named "Antoine." I was like, "Antoine? Wait, yes! I do!" My dad never used his first name. Never liked it much and he thought "Romel Joseph" was more artistic. The man on the line asked me what my relationship to him was. I immediately responded, "His daughter."

He replied, "Your father just arrived at Jackson and he's asking for you before they take him to surgery." About a minute later, he called Bradley, who was sitting next to me, with the same message.

My mother quickly dropped us off since we didn't have a car to get there. Bradley drove and it was quite a ride! I thought my mom was going to get carsick, because he was rushing to get there as fast as he could. I could handle it, but my mom was always dramatic about stuff like that. My cousin, Alex, called as I was on my way, and he told me, "Hey! You're just visiting Jackson, not trying to be a patient there! Haha!" I also called David to let him know what was going on so that he could inform Maestro Marturet of my absence from rehearsal that night. I needed to be with my father.

When Bradley and I arrived at 5:53 p.m., we were greeted by an International Consultant, Sean. He warned us about the graphic nature of walking through a trauma center. We didn't care. All we wanted to do was to be with our father. As we entered, we passed the nurses' station, then I heard my dad! Best sound I could've heard all year!! Bradley was like, "Ah! There is the stomach!" Ha ha. We used to make fun of him because he had a big belly. We immediately recognized him and I quickly went into autopilot.

He literally must've just gotten there because doctors where still assessing how bad his condition was. I walked toward his right side, Bradley on his left. He was groaning as doctors were asking him what hurt. I calmly said, "Pappy, it's me," as I started rubbing his shoulder and arm. He jumped up like a fish out of water! In a raspy voice, he yelled as much as he could.

"Tori! I never thought I'd see you again. Where's Bradley?"

Bradley was in total shock and completely speechless. Bradley said, "I'm here" and followed suit by rubbing his other shoulder.

He said, "Come closer, I want to see you guys!" I noticed his left artificial eye was gone and that his right eye was almost swollen shut, but he did his best to open it as wide as he could. I tried to calm him down. He just kept rambling about how the school was destroyed and how Myslie didn't make it.

In the meantime, the doctors kept asking "Does this hurt?" He would sometimes say "no" and sometimes scream! It wasn't funny, but the way he reacted, then complained made us laugh. Even at his worst, he still had his sense of humor. "These doctors are trying to kill me! They don't want to give me water to drink. My mouth is dry and they won't even let me wet it!"

Bradley and I just kept telling him, "It's going to be okay. You are here now. Don't worry. Things are going to be okay. We are here. You are not alone anymore. Everything is going to be okay."

I couldn't help but observe how bad his feet looked and how bad he looked. His right foot was pretty much sliced open from the ankle to his big toe and it looked VERY deep. His left foot was practically dangling by the ankle and looked like it would fall off if the doctors shook the gurney he was on too much. His whole body was super swollen. Lots of cuts and scrapes. It was hard seeing him like that, but it was definitely better than seeing him in a casket!

Finally, the doctors wanted us to leave so they could wheel him off to surgery. He yelled as loud as he could even though he was super dehydrated, "Give me two minutes! I didn't think I would see my kids again and I want to see my kids!" He negotiated furiously and got his two minutes.

I told him, "Look, you going to have much more than two minutes with us. You need to go so the doctors can fix you up. We're not going anywhere. I promise we will be here when you wake up." I clenched his hand the whole time as he continued to shake his head and calmly responding, "Okay," to everything I was saying.

It was very emotional, but great at the same time. They wheeled him off and Sean took us back to the lobby. As they took him away, I quickly told one of the doctors, "Look, he's legally blind. It's bad enough that he can't see, please do everything you can to save his feet. Don't cut them off! He has a severe complex about being crippled because he's had circulation problems before where he almost lost a foot." He gave me his word that they would do all they could.

Then, Bradley and I hugged for a while. We didn't need to say anything, but we both knew we felt the same thing. Happy, sad, extremely curious, but definitely grateful. Sean then gave me my dad's belongings – his cut-up clothes and his watch. I held on to them wondering what they had been through. I knew in time, my dad would tell me. Bradley and I stayed at the hospital for most of the evening.

At around 9 p.m., they said my dad was available to see visitors. Apparently, he hadn't had surgery yet because the rooms were occupied, so we went to his section of the trauma center where he was waiting for the doctors to pick him up. He seemed more alert and in a better mood then. They cleaned up his wounds as best as they could and wrapped them. He was surrounded by machines to hydrate him and give him much-needed antibiotics.

We spoke briefly, as he was allowed only two visitors at a time. My mother and her husband, Eddie; a family friend, Jolius Tinhomme and his wife, Marlene; and John Arguello and his wife were all waiting to see him, too. It was then that I showed him the contents of his belongings. He didn't care for the clothes, but wanted his watch!

He proceeded to give us a general idea of what happened to him and what he had been through. How he was on the third floor next to his other blind friend, Onickel, delivering a message and fixing the Internet, when the earthquake hit; how he fell three stories into what he described as a "grave," how he was stuck for eighteen hours, etc. We continued to reassure him that he was safe now and in great hands.

After that, we left so other people could visit him. The nurse then told me it would be best for me to go home, as after surgery, he would be in a holding area for a few hours, then assigned to a room, which wouldn't happen till the next day. I left my contact information so that the doctors could reach me, as I am his next of kin. Bradley and I hung out in the trauma center lobby with everyone who came to visit him, then went home.

At around 3 a.m., the doctors called me and explained the severity of his condition as best as they could in a language I could understand. From what I understood, my dad's left foot had broken bones in it. They put an iron fixater on it to readjust the bones to where they need to be and once they were happy with the way it healed, they would remove them so they could put it in a cast. His right foot had no broken bones, but had a huge cut and was also crushed since it was under cement blocks for eighteen hours, so much of the circulation had completely stopped. It would take quite a while to regain feeling in his feet, and it would take even longer for the wound to close since it was so deep.

I didn't realize his left hand was broken since his whole body was swollen, but they told me my dad broke three metacarpals in that hand, which was a big concern for me. I thanked them for saving his feet, as I was sure it would've been easier for them to just cut them off, and then I went to sleep.

Cecilia Johnson

In remembering the emotional days following the January 12th earthquake in Haiti, I think of first reading about the disaster at about 6 p.m. that night on Facebook from a friend that runs a Toledo-based mission to Haiti. I immediately began combing the news on the web and stayed up very late that night worrying.

It wasn't until the next morning, however, that the pictures of the capital building and the surrounding area hit the news and I began to more fully grasp the magnitude of the disaster. The photos of the crumbled palace and numerous buildings in the area brought me to a state of intense worry about Romel and his school. I tried calling via cell phone and could make no connection. Someone on the web mentioned that texting often worked when calls couldn't go through. I knew that Romel's minimal sight would prevent his reading my message, but I sent a text message anyway, with the hope that someone might be able to convey a message to him.

For two days, I worried and had trouble concentrating on much more than Haiti. I spent hours on the computer. I also submitted Romel's name and the school location to the American Red Cross registry. It was on this listing that Romel's ex-wife, Sherry, saw my name and gave me a call. She, too, had heard nothing of Romel's plight and told me of how Victoria and Bradley were sick with worry, with Victoria wanting to fly immediately to Port-au-Prince to try to rescue her dad. The news reports made clear that this would be nearly impossible – at least within the first few days.

Victoria sent me an e-mail about what she knew, and Sherry and I stayed in close touch by phone. I was in the midst of rehearsing for a concert of chamber music that Friday night. I remember feeling in a bit of a daze and even though the concert went well, I was very drained from the emotion of worrying about my friend.

Thursday evening, however, had brought great news. Sherry and I were speaking on the phone when, unbeknownst to us, Romel had managed to get a call through, leaving a message that he was alive, though his legs were broken. Sherry hadn't switched over to his call because she didn't recognize the phone number that had appeared on her cell phone. Immediately after ending our call, she had checked the message and discovered Romel's! She called right away to let me know of his survival.

In the meantime, I had been on Facebook with numerous friends also waiting to hear news of their Haitian friends. There are several very large mission connections to Haiti from Toledo. When I had returned from visiting Romel's school about five years ago, I had become involved with fundraising for Haiti through these various groups.

I had become somewhat disheartened about our local newspaper's *(Toledo Blade)* coverage of the earthquake on the morning following the disaster. It received only second page notice. I sent an e-mail to our new editor of the *Blade* asking about this.

Several days later, and after much more complete coverage, he sent a reply asking if I was satisfied with the reporting. I answered him saying that I was, and decided to tell him a little bit about Romel. He asked if I might tell Romel's story to a former writer of the *Blade* who now wrote for the *Miami Herald,* Mike Sallah. I agreed and spoke with Mike for several days as Romel arrived for treatment in Miami. His story was one, I felt, that should be heard. My instincts told me that if his story were told, warm hearts out in the world might be willing to help him. I was very happy that as things transpired, this proved to be true. What a whirlwind week for Romel as he became a national celebrity. I was amazed by the poise and graciousness that he showed in speaking to the national audience.

As things have continued, Romel and I have stayed in touch via phone. I began speaking to friends in various organizations and at church. I started talking to the students at Adrian College (where I have taught for years) about Romel and his school. The students decided to put on a benefit concert for his school.

Simultaneously, Adrian College alum Eric Swanson had gathered together other alums for a double benefit concert, one in Adrian and one in Detroit. When Eric heard about Romel's school, he decided to put all of the proceeds toward it, rather than in a general fund for Haiti. These concerts took place on February 26th and 27th. Approximately $3000 was raised.

Shar Products of Ann Arbor, Michigan also agreed to send violin outfits to help replace the musical instruments that were destroyed in the earthquake.

THE MIRACLE OF MUSIC

The rebuilding process is now in its planning stages, but my friendship with Romel is one that will last a lifetime. I plan to support Romel's efforts for many years to come!

Sherry Joseph

My experience

A couple years ago, my two children, Victoria and Bradley, asked me how it felt to be a half-century old. That thought was quite staggering and I was so dumbfounded, I could not formulate a response. That same year, my grandmother passed away at the ripe old age of 101. I cannot begin to fathom the number of experiences she had in her life, nor can I imagine where she stored all those memories. In all honesty, I have forgotten many events that I have experienced in my fifty-two years on this earth.

Certain ones, however, are indelible as ink; they are permanently tattooed in my mind. I still remember exactly where I was sitting in my second grade class when the school principal made the announcement over the PA system that President Kennedy had been assassinated. The same holds true for that tragic morning of September 11th, 2001, when terrorists hijacked the four planes and attacked the World Trade Center and the Pentagon. I recall sitting at my desk in the basement of Barry University Library and receiving a phone call from a colleague who told me of the events.

The plane crash in Shanksville, Pennsylvania, which is about fifty miles from where I am originally from and where my parents still reside to this day, was incomprehensible. Years later, I visited the crash site. The third and fourth memories which are etched in my mind forever include all the events surrounding the destruction of The New Victorian School in Haiti, first from a fire on January 12th, 2000, and then from the earthquake on January 12th of this year.

I spent nearly twenty years of my life in the country of Haiti. Initially, I went there as a missionary. After I completed my four-year contract, I elected to stay on and work as a volunteer at St. Vincent's School for Handicapped Children. I had lived there for nearly five months while I was in language school, and I loved being with the children who helped me perfect my Creole and taught me so much about living life to fullest in spite of physical handicaps.

It was there that I also met Romel, who was the Director of Music. The school is under the auspices of the Episcopal Church, and was founded by Sister Joan Margaret, SSM, a dynamic woman who beat cancer three times and lived to be ninety-nine years old. Sister Joan was the same age as my grandmother and just as nurturing. I valued her opinions and advice more than anyone in this world. Her wisdom was comparable to that of King Solomon.

When Romel and I became engaged, she told me there were three kinds of men that women should NEVER marry – doctors, Episcopal priests, and musicians. Their professions involve such irregular work schedules that can place a strain on marriage. Nevertheless, I married Romel, and embarked on a life that was anything but dull!

Our first two years of married life were spent in New York City where Romel completed his master's degree at The Juilliard School of Music. I was incredibly fortunate to find employment at St. Joseph's College in Brooklyn, across the street from the meager studio apartment we rented. Once Romel completed his degree, we returned to St. Vincent's and assumed our same roles as Director of Music and Personal Assistant to Sister Joan, respectively.

Shortly after our return, our daughter Victoria was born. We resided at St. Vincent's for another year and then moved to Avenue N, #13, the physical address of The New Victorian School. I remember one of our fellow volunteers at St. Vincent's asking me if we were superstitious about the number "13" in our address. At the time, I wasn't; now, I have second thoughts.

When it came time for Victoria to go to school, life in Haiti was politically unstable. In order to ensure little or no interruption in her studies, we decided to create our own school and name it after her. The Victorian School was scheduled to open its doors on September 30th, 1991. On the eve of that date, there was a coup d'état and President Jean Bertrand Aristide was forced to go into exile. Of the twelve students who enrolled in the school, nine left for the States, never to return. In October, we opened the doors of The Victorian School with three students, one being Victoria.

The school grew rapidly and by the year 2000, we had over 150 students enrolled in preschool to 6th grade. In addition, there was an Early Bird section offering ESL (English as a Second Language) for children. The Joseph family had experienced some personal problems, but everything was on the mend and we had relocated to Miami. Bradley, who was four years old at the time, and I were traveling back and forth on a monthly basis to make sure the school was running properly.

On the afternoon of January 12th, 2000, at approximately 5 p.m., the phone rang. Romel took the call; it was from Tanya Desamours, one of his former violin students and a close friend.

The reason for her phone call was devastating – and as Romel was about to break the news to me, I simply spoke one word, "Fire." Romel gave me a puzzled look as if to say, "How did you know?" I went on to share something that I had never told him prior to that moment.

For nearly six months, I had been experiencing a recurring image of flames. I had NO idea what the image meant, so I never shared it with anyone. At the exact moment that Tanya called, I was in the kitchen washing dishes. Once again, I saw the flames. Then, it was very clear to me. It was the school, completely destroyed by what we believe was a power surge which caused sparks in the kitchen where there was a propane gas tank for the stove.

Romel and I quickly made arrangements for the children and boarded a plane for Port-au-Prince the following day. His sister picked us up at the airport and took us to the school which was nothing more than a smoldering pile of debris. We learned that firefighters had actually responded to the fire, arriving on the scene with their fire trucks but NO water. Ultimately, a Victorian School parent who was employed at the National Palace had sent a fire truck back there to get one load of water to extinguish the final flames.

Although we had lost everything, there was no loss of life. I remember meeting the employees that day and asking God to give me the right words to say. I told them, "The fire has caused us to take two steps backward; now we must take three steps forward." It took several years, but Romel did just that. He painstakingly took those three steps forward and rebuilt the school. There was never a question of his dedication and commitment to the schoolchildren. School reopened two weeks after the fire and little by little, The NEW Victorian School took shape.

Sometimes life takes twists and turns that we can never foresee or prevent from happening. I was disenchanted with the frequent travel and school. My educational training empowered me to be an outstanding instructor, but left me frustrated as an administrator. Similarly, Romel was struggling with issues in the Miami Dade County Public School System. We agreed to change places and I took a full time position as an ESL instructor on the campus of Barry University. He assumed the leadership of The New Victorian School. Over time, we drifted apart. We no longer shared the same interests, and we disagreed about the children and their choices.

Romel created a new life for himself in Haiti. I went back to grad school and accomplished the master's degree in leadership that I had put off for more than twenty-five years. We divorced in September 2006, after twenty-one years of marriage. Yes, it was bitter, and it hurt more than I could ever imagine, but it caused the tension and competition between us to abate. Within no time, we cultivated a friendship and a bond that will last forever.

All this brings me to the events of January 12th of this year. I had finished working at 3 p.m. My fiancé, Eddie, and I were on our way to pick up some computer supplies in South Miami. We were traveling down US 1, and since Eddie was driving, I decided to take a nap after a busy day at work. My phone beeped, and I woke up, irritated because I felt as if someone had stolen my reverie. I noticed that we had reached Coral Gables and were in front of the University of Miami Campus. When I looked at my phone, Victoria's number showed up. I remember thinking how ironic her timing was, because she was a senior at the University of Miami. I also remember thinking that something must be wrong because Victoria never calls; she only sends text messages.

Groggily, I took the call. Victoria was extremely distressed. She asked if I had heard the news. "What news?" I said. She then proceeded to tell me about the earthquake in Port-au-Prince and her concerns for her father and the school. I tried to calm her down, telling her how structurally sound the school was with all the reinforcement iron. We ended the conversation there and promised to keep in touch if either of us heard anything.

After telling Eddie the news, I decided to call my mother in Pennsylvania. The area in which she resides seems to get a lot of news from Haiti and I thought maybe she would know something. Indeed, she had the news on and told me that there was minimal damage to the National Palace. My parents have visited Haiti on four separate occasions as part of short-term work crews for the same mission I worked for. They were extremely familiar with Haiti.

Mom's words were somewhat comforting, so I called Tori (Victoria) back to let her know. I had personally witnessed the majority of the school construction; it was so well-fortified with reinforcement iron that I felt that even if it were damaged it would still be standing. During my years in Haiti, I remember experiencing three very mild earthquakes, and nothing consequential ever happened. Eddie and I continued on our way to South Miami.

While we were in the store, I went to the section with laptops. I found one that was connected to the Internet and I began searching for news about Haiti. There were several articles entitled "Breaking News," but there were no pictures. Because the quake occurred shortly before 5 p.m., it was already dark in Port-au-Prince. I remember a salesman approaching me to offer his assistance. I told him that my ex-husband was in Haiti and I was trying to find information about the earthquake. He told me he understood and that he would pray for Romel's safety. It was very heartwarming. Eddie and I went home. He bought a couple phone cards on the way in hope that we could make contact with the school.

The next morning, I awoke to the terrifying realization that on January 12th, 2000, the school was destroyed by fire, and exactly ten years to the very day, almost to the very same time, the school was hit by an earthquake. I shared this with Eddie; however, I decided not to bring up the subject with Tori or Bradley at the time. Both children were already overwrought since no one had heard from Romel. At that point, I believe we were all running on automatic pilot.

It was difficult to go to work that day. As the GED Program Coordinator for Miami Dade College, Wolfson Campus, I am involved with individuals who have distractions due to hardship almost daily. That day, I made many apologies to my students for my own distraction. In the afternoon, after the staff meeting, I went home to rest and be with Eddie.

Talking to Eddie was comforting and helped me sort things out. We both felt that with each passing hour, the chances of Romel's survival decreased. Eddie accessed some high-resolution aerial photographs of Port-au-Prince. Things did not look good. I began following Richard Morse on Twitter. Richard and his wife, Lunise, operate the Oloffson Hotel which is just blocks away from The New Victorian School. In fact, their children, Isabelle and William, attended the school years ago.

By Thursday, I told Tori that she should "tweet" Richard and see if he could send someone to the school and check on her father. I continued to search the Internet for any information I could find, all the time keeping my phone next to me. At some point, and to be honest, I cannot recall exactly when, I told Eddie that if Romel was alive, that he would contact me first. To me, it was only logical – I was the one who is most reliable in terms of answering my phone. Deep in my heart, I honestly felt that Romel was alive, but I never voiced that thought, mainly because I was afraid I might be wrong.

On Thursday evening, after class, I was searching more sites on the web. I e-mailed the American Embassy in Port-au-Prince, knowing that Romel was a United States citizen and part of the Warden's Network in Haiti. While I was searching on the Red Cross site, Romel's name came up. His information was placed there by Cecilia Johnson, from Toledo, Ohio.

Cecilia and Romel both attended the University of Cincinnati Conservatory of Music back in the 1980s. She had helped raise funds for The New Victorian School after the fire, and she had even visited the school to attend one of the graduation ceremonies. Cecilia had entered her contact information in hopes of receiving word about Romel. After the divorce, I had lost contact with her, so I quickly grabbed my phone and dialed her number. Her husband Erick answered, and after I told him who I was, he quickly passed the phone to Cecilia. I didn't have any news to give her, but I promised that as soon as I did, I would call or e-mail. She was so pleased that we had re-established contact, and promised to pray for Romel and his wife, Myslie.

While Cecilia and I were talking, I received another call on my phone. It was from Marie Saintus. I chose to ignore the call for two reasons. First, I really didn't want to interrupt my conversation with Cecilia. Secondly, Marie Saintus was an individual I had met earlier that week in my GED class. I was annoyed because

I could not understand how she had acquired my personal cell phone number.

When Cecilia and I hung up, I listened to my voice mail. The message was from Romel! His voice was raspy and somewhat difficult to understand, but he at least he was able to let us know that he was alive. I switched my phone to speaker and played it for Eddie, and then Bradley. I sent Tori a text message and then proceeded to call Cecilia back. Romel was almost incomprehensible, but after listening to the message several times, we were able to make out that he was all right, but Myslie did not make it. The school was destroyed. He also said that he would need a lot of help with the upcoming Walenstein concert.

Once the level of excitement died down, I tried to call Marie Saintus. She did not pick up. Anger reared its bitter head. How dare this woman do this to me! After all, I really tried to be helpful to her on Monday when she came to class.

Permit me to just back up for a moment. Walt Disney is credited with the theme, "It's a Small World." My encounter with Marie Saintus fits into that category. However, more appropriately, I believe it perfectly fits the old adage which states, "The Lord works in mysterious ways." Marie came to my afternoon GED Preparation classes on Monday, January 11th. She is visually impaired. My lab facilities had only two very outdated programs which do not work well with my GED Prep software. One of my very talented students tried to help Marie.

Ultimately, when the computer monitor was just too small for her, Marie asked me if we had an online program she could follow. Her own computer equipment was more sophisticated and she would be able to function normally. I immediately made a phone call and Marie was transferred to online classes. I told her to keep in touch and let me know if she experienced any problems or required further assistance on my part. Case closed, or so I thought....

Now, just how did Marie get my cell phone number? I never give it out to any student. The next morning, Friday at approximately 6:15 a.m., I was a woman on a mission. I called Marie's number again and left a message. In a firm voice full of conviction, I told her that I was Romel's ex-wife and the mother of his two children. If anyone had a right to know what was going on, it was me. I also reminded her of the assistance I had provided for her earlier in the week. In essence, I was begging her to call and give me any information she had.

Within a few moments, Marie called. We spoke for nearly forty-five minutes. I learned that she has known Romel for over thirty-five years; she was married to one of his closest friends, Maurice. Maurice was also visually handicapped and played the trumpet. He passed away several years ago. He and Marie have two children. I also learned that she did radio broadcasts with Onickel Augustin and Romel. All of them had grown up at St. Vincent's because of their visual impairments. At that time, I was reminded of just how efficient that "blind" network was.

Marie shared with me that she was able to get the call out from Onickel's cell phone. She also told me that Romel's legs were broken, but he was all right. For two nights, both he and Onickel had been sleeping in cars. With all the aftershocks, it was not safe to be inside a building. She felt that both men were downplaying their injuries in order for all of us not to worry. I thanked Marie profusely for all her efforts in putting Romel in touch with us. She was so gracious and modest; she was just a servant doing God's work. The last piece of news she had was that both Onickel and Romel were going to be airlifted back to the States later that day.

After hanging up, I quickly gave the news to Bradley, who then called Tori. From there, I began making other calls to let family, friends, and colleagues know that our prayers had been answered. Later that day, while both children were at my apartment, they received phone calls from Ryder Trauma Center. They wanted us at the hospital immediately. I dropped the children there and went to meet Eddie, who was nearby, but experiencing car problems. The kids were to call a coordinator who would meet them at the entrance to the hospital. In my mind, I figured things must be really bad – first Ryder Trauma and then a personal coordinator or counselor.

Tori called me immediately, completely distraught by her father's condition. I tried to remain as calm and composed as possible. I remember telling her that if her father made it that far, he would undoubtedly make it the rest of the way. Eddie and I quickly got the car taken care of, and went back to the hospital. There we found the children as well as John and Laura Arguello. John was a piano instructor for Romel's program for many years. Romel had been taken into the operating room so doctors could begin to clean up his wounds and assess the damage.

Later, someone came out and told us that two people could go in and see Romel. I sent the children in first. When they came out, Eddie and I briefly went in to see him. He was very swollen, and his voice was full of fatigue, despair, and disorientation. We tried to be reassuring and strong for him, but it was not an easy job. We left in order that John and Laura could spend a few minutes with him also, before Romel went back into surgery. It was the first of many to follow. Eddie and I went home. More phone calls, more prayers, and some much-needed rest after several sleepless nights.

Just prior to the earthquake, Romel had called me to discuss the future of his programs with me. He outlined some expectations and asked me to consider a one-year contract to help Walenstein. I discussed it with Eddie and then accepted the offer. At that time, I never knew it would transform into this. Eddie and I were married on Valentine's Day. Romel's situation caused us to think about life and how uncertain it can be. In all, it feels good and it feels right. People ask us how we can do it – my husband and I now help out my ex-. We are mature adults who put the past behind us and focus on the future. Hopefully, we will be an example for others.

Back to my story. When I woke up the next day, I touched my left foot, and I couldn't believe what I felt. It was some kind of iron which was inserted in five places in my left foot. "What is this?" I asked.

The nurse answered, "It's an iron fixater which is designed to hold the bones of your foot in place.

I replied, "It feels like something that children in kindergarten would design for their artwork."

The nurse said, "I don't know, but that's what your foot needs at this time."

I was always so afraid of hospitals that I used to avoid walking near one so I wouldn't end up in one. Now here I am. It was my first time being resident of a hospital since I was four years old, and I wasn't prepared for the experience. But God had other plans. I was going to be a resident in one for a long time.

For the first few days, I was constantly being visited by friends and family members. Some of the members of Emais Baptist Church who are affiliated with Walenstein Musical Organization came and prayed for me. My phone was loaded with calls by friends from everywhere in the US.

The next thing I knew, a reporter from the *Miami Herald*, Mr. Mike Sallah, came in my room. He told me that he was connected to someone who is a friend of Cecilia's, and he wanted to do a story on me; and that was done. The next morning, it was Katie Couric from CBS, then next came CNN, then *The Washington Post*, etc. From then on, almost every day I had an interview. I have no idea how I was able to give these interviews since I was on so much pain medicine. I could barely finish a sentence. My throat was always dry, and my voice was so raspy.

The situation, however, wasn't too pleasant for my roommate because there was too much going on in the section of my room. Between all the visitors, phone calls, late night visits from family, it was always noisy. Hence, I was moved to a private room. I was really happy about that. But after a few days, I was increasingly having lots and lots of problems in the hospital.

My left hand had a cast. So consequently, I needed someone to bathe me, to feed me hospital food which I could hardly eat, and to help me go to the bathroom, which I hated so much. I was bored to death, lying on my back in between four walls doing nothing, for I am a highly active person. This particular problem was alleviated when the Lighthouse for the Blind lent me a computer and Stevie Wonder gave me a keyboard. I remember one evening, there was a really loud train nearby that woke me up and I thought it was an earthquake. A nurse walking by had to come in and calm me down.

In addition, students from music schools would come and play for me. And that was really pleasant and soothing. I also couldn't sleep at night because every hour, the nurses would come to check my vital signs. Finally, I asked that they stay out of my room between midnight and 6:00 a.m. so that I could sleep, which they mostly did.

But my greatest problem was Myslie. For the first four weeks, especially while I watched the news, I saw people who were being removed from shattered buildings after many days. I started to think that Myslie might still be alive and somehow if I could leave the hospital and go to Haiti, I might still have a chance to save her. But that wasn't going to happen, for there was no way that the doctors would let me leave the hospital. That made me extremely frustrated and angry.

I would get mad at the nurses for any little thing and would have to apologize to them later. These nurses were highly professional and understanding; and I think they somehow knew what I was going through. I had to ask constantly for pain medicine, for the pain was mostly unbearable.

I was always hungry at night. Luckily, Victoria would come virtually every night to bring me food from outside and to make sure I had everything I needed, as well as Sherry, my friend Michou, and Nicole. The biggest obstacle though I had to overcome during my days in the hospital was to go to the hyperbaric chamber treatments.

I also had a lot of problems with the wound bandages changes for my right foot. At first, they would change it twice a day, which was horrifying! My foot was extremely sensitive. Any slight touch was excruciating. It was as if someone was slicing my foot like they were searing a fish fillet – very slowly! The cut was so deep that it felt like they were stuffing teddy bears with all the gauze they put inside my foot. Taking it out was no walk in the park either! As my foot got better, they would change it once a day, then once every two days,

THE MIRACLE OF MUSIC

One morning, a group of doctors dressed in white came to my room. Their appearance in my room usually scared me because when a group of people dressed in white are coming to you, especially while you are waking up, it means that death is coming for you. But they were real doctors.

One of the doctors said, "Good morning Mr. Joseph, how are you today?"

I replied, "Good morning, Doctors. I am okay. Thanks. Is there something I need to know?"

The doctor said, "Yes. In order to speed up your healing process, you will need to go a few times to the hyperbaric chamber."

"What is that?" I asked.

The doctor said, "It's a chamber where you will breathe pure oxygen, which will help your feet heal in order for us to do a skin graft on them."

I said, "Okay. That should be fine."

So the arrangements were made, and I was taken the next day to the hyperbaric chamber. This chamber is a small rectangular box that takes you down somewhere, and you have to either sit, or lie down for two hours while they put a mask on your face to breathe the oxygen.

This first visit was a nightmare for me. I felt like I was under the ground and this time, my face was locked up. I couldn't do it. So the next day, the doctors came to me again.

The doctor said, "We learned that you had a bad experience in the hyperbaric chamber."

"Yes. I am claustrophobic and it feels like I am back under the ground."

"If you do not receive this treatment, we will not be able to take care of your feet."

"You mean my feet might be amputated?" I asked.

"We might have to," the doctor said.

The doctors and I discussed this matter extensively. I tried to ask for an alternative treatment to help my feet heal faster, but they insisted that hyperbaric was the best option they had. It was either I go, or they cut off my feet. So we came up with a compromise.

I said, "I guess I must find a way to be in that room. What if you give me a sedative ten minutes before I enter the room so I can sleep? And maybe someone could be sitting near me so that I don't feel alone?"

The doctor said, "Okay. We will prescribe a sedative for that purpose."

My suggestions worked and I was able to go to the hyperbaric chamber fourteen times, and they were able to do the skin graft.

Every week, I had to have more surgeries to help clean the wounds on both my feet. I always dreaded it since I would be under full anesthesia. That, and the fact that I don't like surgery. Every Thursday was "surgery day" and both Bradley and Victoria would come by afterwards and spend the night with me since they were the hardest days. I would be so groggy from the anesthesia, starving because I couldn't eat or drink the night before, and it was always nice not to be alone for the evening. If there is one thing that I have learned from this experience is that it's not advisable for anyone to stay in a hospital without a family member or a great friend.

As time went on, more interviews happened. Stevie Wonder donated his personal keyboard to me, which was truly remarkable.

THE MIRACLE OF MUSIC

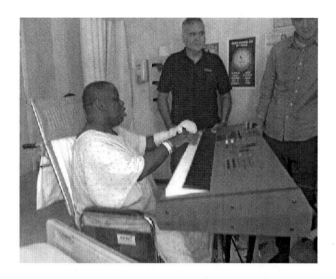

Several wonderful people came to visit me, played for me, and donated their instruments to the school. The hyperbaric treatments, wound changes, and surgeries continued.

On February 23, 2010, the cast on my left hand was finally removed. I had surgery to have pins placed on the bones of my pinky, ring finger, and middle finger, between my wrists and knuckles.

On March 4th, I finally had my skin graft procedure. They took a piece of skin from my left thigh and covered what would now be the skin above both my right and left inner ankle bones.

Finally, on March 6th, I was discharged from the hospital and sent to Jackson Rehabilitation Center. They tried to keep me there for weeks, but I was ready to leave the hospital and return to Haiti. I told them to instruct me on what I needed to do so I could practice during that time in order to be discharged more quickly. I was out by a week and was sent home on March 13th to be under home care.

ROMEL JOSEPH

Right away, I scheduled my first trip to travel with Victoria on March 29th to clean up the debris and find Myslie and the maid who were still under the rubble.

I tried to prepare myself emotionally as best as I could, for I knew these coming days were going to be emotionally difficult. Sherry and her husband, Eddie, got me a wheelchair. I still had the iron fixater on my left foot, and I knew that I was going to be highly susceptible to infections in my feet, so I had to be very careful with it. Thank goodness I could hop on my right foot, which made me somewhat mobile.

Right before the trip on March 25th, the BBC came to be with me for a documentary which was to be on TV on July 12th, 2010. We also had a wonderful fundraising concert for The New Victorian School on March 27th at the Broward Center for Performing Arts. There were many wonderful artists, including the eight-year-old violinist Briana Kahane, whom I first met when she came in the hospital in February to play for me. She gave to The New Victorian School the first violin that she owned. There was the great violinist Ida Haendel, and many others who performed for that musical event.

Finally, on Monday, March 29th, Victoria and I were off to Haiti.

9

Returning to Haiti, Finding Myslie, Rebuilding, Following My New Life Mission.

On March 29th, I woke up really early, around 8 a.m., anxious and at the same time highly excited. The day had come for me to go to Haiti for the first time since the earthquake. I wasn't sure what to expect or how much work was going to be needed.

Victoria had made all the necessary arrangements with her schedule so that she could go with me, which was a Godsend, and I was really excited about the fact that she was coming along. I knew with the delicate condition of my feet and my health in general, I would need her to especially help me to avoid dangerous infections.

Victoria, Bradley, and I did some last-minute packing; then we went to Walgreens to get some pain medicine. Then, we went to the airport. Arriving there, we had difficulty finding someone to help us with the suitcases, which was kind of frustrating. Finally, we were helped by some security officers. All went well checking in, and going through security.

ROMEL JOSEPH

Once we got to the gate, I asked the American Airlines people who were responsible for boarding that if, by chance, there was an empty place in first class since that's where I was seated due to the fact that I needed more leg room, could my daughter come and sit with me? They totally refused. It would have really helped, for I had tremendous pain during the flight because of the air pressure. The left leg was draining through the places were the iron entered in the different parts in my leg and foot. The right foot was seeping even worse.

Victoria, who is a massage therapist, could have really helped. What was sad is that there were many empty seats in first class, and people near me were willing to move to other seats so my daughter could come and assist me. But the flight attendants refused any change whatsoever. The man next to me, Mr. Rendell Brewster, who was like my guardian angel on the flight, also tried to help me to convince these flight attendants, but we both failed. I feel that they were being truly inhumane.

THE MIRACLE OF MUSIC

Arriving in Port-au-Prince, I waited for everyone to get off the flight, and then a man with a wheelchair came and picked me up. We went outside and to my great surprise, a bus came to take the other passengers and me to immigration because the earthquake had destroyed part of the airport. It felt like getting on the airport train in Miami. Then we arrived in baggage claim and customs. The heat was incredible because the building is covered with a roof made of tin. I analyzed how it was constructed and it gave me many ideas about how to build something similar for the temporary shelter of The New Victorian School.

People at the airport were looking at me as if I came from another planet, because of the condition of my feet. The situation was even more pronounced once we went outside. I was surrounded by people who were asking me questions about my medical condition, and especially about my earthquake story. Then came a camionette which picked me up to take me to the Doux Sejour Hotel in Petionville, where I decided to stay during this trip in order to sleep away from infected areas, and mainly for safety reasons.

I wasn't sure how safe the school was, and especially due to the condition of my feet, I didn't want to expose them to high level of contamination. My driver Marcel, the guardian of the school, Ladouceur, and my sister-in-law Josette came to pick me up. The camionette driver, who is a friend of my driver, was really nice, though his truck was giving all kinds of problems and it had to be pushed several times to get it started.

We finally arrived at Madame Micheline Denis's house, my pianist since 1983. She was the one who made the reservation for me at Doux Sejour Hotel, which is located on the same street as her house. She was really happy to see me, but when she saw my feet, she wasn't able to believe what she saw, and she said my feet grossed her out. She told us where the hotel was and we went there.

It's a small hotel in a family style, and a house. Once arriving there, we checked in, and we were taken to our room which was very nice. The hotel is not really handicapped accessible, but I decided to stay there anyway for a few days. I asked Josette to stay with us in the hotel and she accepted. She was an excellent help to me and Victoria. She assisted in everything I needed, including cleaning up, doing laundry, making phone calls, and helping me get to bathroom -- she functioned like walker so I could hold on to her while she held on to me. We really had a nice first day, and were anticipating tomorrow which would be our first day of work.

The next day, March 30th, we got up kind of early; around 7:00 a.m., had breakfast around 8:00, and then we went to Hinet, which is a very popular Internet company. But we were not able to obtain an Internet connection because they didn't have an Internet box which would have allowed us to have Internet anywhere we were. We were not too happy, but we knew we had to accept the situation.

Because it was kind of difficult for me to get off at every stop, I had to decide where I should get out of the car. At some places, such as Hinet or Sogebel (the bank), customer service officers would come out and talk to me because they had too many stairs, which was impractical. Other places such as Camcel, a cell phone company, had a ramp for handicapped. Other places such as Unicarte would not make it too easy for me. My driver had to take care of my transactions with great difficulty. I was frequently observed by a small crowd everywhere I went.

Then we spent some time, visiting Port-au-Prince, especially around the National Palace and downtown.

I couldn't believe what I saw once I arrived in front of Holy Trinity as well as St. Vincent's School. There was nothing but empty space in these two places where I spent most of my life growing up and working. I guess I got really emotional and cried, especially when I learned of the great number of people who died in both institutions. Seeing how bad things were in these places gave me courage to walk into The New Victorian School, knowing that things could have been worse.

As I was going to The New Victorian School, we drove in front of Doctor Leslie Paul-Pierre's clinic and he was sitting right there in front of his office. I asked the driver to stop the car and with lots of excitement, I called to him. He said, "I remember you." I told him that I stopped to thank him for taking care of me on the street when I came out of the ground. He looked at my feet and said that my doctor did a great job.

I explained to him my story from the time I left him on January 13th and he was totally happy for me and we took a picture together. He had spent the last three months taking care of earthquake victims like me, free of charge. In time, when I am financially more stable, I hope to contribute to his mission of helping others. I also suggested to him that he start a nonprofit medical institution in order to have more possibilities to assist the citizens of Haiti. Then we went to The New Victorian School.

ROMEL JOSEPH

Because we know that the level of dust would be high, I put a pillowcase on each foot. In doing so, I hoped to prevent the dirt as well as the flies from getting in to my wounds. As I was getting out of the car, all my friends and employees came to the car door to greet me instead of waiting for me to get in the school. They were so happy to see me, and I was just as happy to see them. Some of them were in shock, crying; others were praising God because he saved my life and brought me back to Haiti. I felt so loved.

Then I got to the school gate. I was shocked. I could not believe what I saw -- the way the different floors of the building fell on each other. Boss Sonson, the man who saved me, showed me where I was. For some time, I was speechless and in shock. It was a true miracle that anyone was saved from the collapse of the building.

THE MIRACLE OF MUSIC

I spent over three hours meeting with the different administrators and teachers, looking at the possibility to restart school on
April 12th, or April 19th. But the work to clean the yard would be
immense. However, we hoped we would be able to complete it. I
also had a short interview with the *London Times* that afternoon.
In short, it was a fruitful and emotional day.

In the evening, around 6:00, Madame Denis and her husband
came to visit me. I was so happy to see them. We spent some time
talking about music and concerts, and I told her that I wanted
to build a performing arts center in Haiti and I would like Mr.
Benjamin, a violinist, architect, and engineer to design and build
it. She told me that he would not be interested because he worked
for us between 1995 and 1996 -- during most of that time I was
in the States, and he had a bad experience with my wife and me.
I sent him a letter and hoped he would accept my apology and
participate in the plan.

On March 31st, Victoria spent some time in a cyber café, and
then we went to the American Embassy. As we were going there,
we got a flat tire. Luckily this happened right in front of a tire repair shop. This was more luck than good management. My driver
left the tire to be fixed and put on the spare, and we continued on
our way to the embassy.

Once we got there, the security officers asked us what we
wanted; I responded that I needed to go to the USAID office
for information. They told me that I was in the right place. They
made me speak to an officer; I told him that I needed one USAID
truck from all of these which were all over the city to help me
clean up the rubble at the school. The response was: "We don't
know anything about what you are talking about," and that was
that.

So, we went to ACS -- the American Citizen Service. It was lunch time. So I was connected by phone with a lady. I made the same request as before, and she said, "The United States Embassy does not offer that kind of service to US citizens because there are too many of them in the country."

I insisted, "But I have a school with American citizens and I am an American citizen, and schools have priority."

She said, "Then talk to your Haitian government."

Again I insisted, "I have an American passport; doesn't that make me an American citizen?"

She replied, "I can't help you. Send an e-mail to this address: acspap@state.gov."

I said, "Thank you," and left.

Considering that the American people, through all forms of fundraising events, gave over two billion dollars to help with the earthquake situation, and Presidents Bush and Clinton have raised so much money for this purpose, I thought that school-children would have been among the beneficiaries. But obviously that wasn't the case.

Following my trip to the embassy, I decided to go to Digicel, Hitel, and Camcel, the three cell phone companies which also offered Internet service using a card. But due to the earthquake, they had suspended new service, and we were having all kinds of problems getting access to the Internet. The hotel supposedly had Internet, but it was so slow that it was virtually impossible to use it.

Then I went to the school. The employees were working furiously. There was dust everywhere. Consequently, I had to have lunch on the street sidewalk, in the car, across the street from the school, where one of my employees had cooked a delicious lunch for Tori and me. We were surrounded by several of the teachers who were conversing with us while we ate. It was truly pleasant and nice to be back to Haiti, away from the hospital's lonely life.

On April 1st, not much happened. We got up late; around 9:00 a.m., because the driver had to go service the car early in the morning. Around 9:30, Rev. David Cesar, an Anglican priest who was the director of the Holy Trinity music department and a violist, came to visit us with two other orchestra members. We spent almost two hours sharing our stories of the earthquake and talking about the role that music, particularly classical music, should have in the future of the new Haiti, and especially how we could all work together.

Then, around noon, we went to Madame Denis' house for a short visit, which was really fun. They were afraid of my getting out of the car, so they all came outside to talk to me. Following this visit, we drove to the school. I spent the rest of the afternoon observing the people who were removing the rubble. Both Victoria and I served as motivating forces to keep them working. They had removed lots of debris and they were nearing my room. I was getting a little more nervous. It wouldn't be long before we would find Myslie.

Her sister had been with me for the past four days, helping me as a caretaker and assistant, but she would go home to be with her family for the next days. Two of her brothers worked in the cleaning up process. I think they were really there waiting to find their sister who, as I learned last night, was financially responsible for them. Such a surprise! I never could tell why her money used to disappear so fast. I thought she had a boyfriend she was taking care of.

On April 3rd, the first thing I did around 12:30 a.m. was to call Bradley to wish him a happy eighteenth birthday and lots of success as he enters the adult world. I promised him that I would be with him every step of the way, but all decisions would have to be his, for it was his life. Then around 10:00 a.m., we went to the store to purchase a huge gallon of Clorox and masks for the workers to put on their faces as they approached the two ladies who died underground: my maid and my wife. We arrived at the school around 11:00 a.m.

Some of the teachers came to visit and observe the work that was going on. Many had not only lost family members but also their houses. And of course each individual just like me, with a dramatic story to tell about how he/she was saved from the earthquake.

On April 5th, we started early, around 8:30 a.m. We went first to Access Haiti to pay for the Internet service for a friend of Onickel's who is presently out of town for a few days -- she allowed us to use her wireless Internet as long as we agreed to pay the service fee for the month of April, which is $60 US. We were happy to start having contact with the world via the Internet. Onickel had made this arrangement for us since I was complaining to him about how we were not able to communicate with people in the States.

Then we went to see Marie Laurance Lassegue, the Minister of Culture, at the suggestion of my friend Raoul Denis Jr., who called her and left a message on her answering machine. But apparently she didn't listen to her messages and didn't know I was coming.

Once I arrived there on Monday, March 5th, she made me wait for two hours. I was getting really frustrated. So I drove my wheelchair to the door of her office "tent" and I said loudly enough for her to hear, "It was really difficult for me to come here, and I don't have much time."

She replied, "I am busy too myself, and you didn't make an appointment."

I insisted, "It will take only two minutes."

She replied, "You didn't have an appointment."

I then called my friend Raoul Denis and told him, "I am right in front of her tent door and she said that she will not talk to me." We managed to get into her tent, and Victoria gave her the phone. She came outside while talking on the phone. She told my friend that he shouldn't send anyone to see her on Mondays, because she was always too busy.

Following the conversation, she looked at me, puzzled, and said, "Did the earthquake do that to you?"

I said, "Yes, it did." I am assuming that looking at me, she understood why I couldn't wait in the sun for hours. Then she said, "Come tomorrow at 10:00 a.m. and I will meet with you." I thanked her, and drove away.

Then I went to the school. The workers found my maid, who died under the building. One of my oldest workers who is a carpenter came, and I hired him to build two coffins. He made one that afternoon, which would be used for the maid, Selita. And then he started the other for my wife, Myslie, who was still not yet found.

I was nervous about the whole funeral situation. My stomach had been queasy since the previous night, to the point where I was vomiting in the morning. The stress was catching up to me; especially since Myslie's mother came to town this afternoon and would be with us in the school for the next three days.

Due to financial limitations, I couldn't hire a funeral parlor to take care of the burials. As a result, I had to deal with the dreadful details. I would need a specialist who knew how to carry dead people and a truck driver willing to carry two bodies. Then, I had to hire a spirit expert to liberate their souls so they wouldn't hang around the school scaring the children, and go to their resting place in peace. Next, I had to find a space in the cemetery where both can be laid to rest, get a death certificate for Myslie, and especially pay attention to what Josette told me about not going to the cemetery with my dead wife, so she wouldn't persecute any other girl I may have in the future. That was VERY important.

In addition, according to Haitian custom, I had to wear red, especially at night, so that Myslie's spirit wouldn't try to continue the relationship, which I don't really believe. Myslie even told me that herself once. "When I die," she said, "you better wear red at night or else I'll come and find you."

April 6th, 2010 was a productive day. Around 9:00 a.m., my driver and I went to put out announcements for a parents' meeting which would take place on April 9th at 7:30 a.m., as well as an announcement of the need for two elementary teachers for the French section of the school due to the death of two of our teachers. Simultaneously, Victoria went to cyber café to make some photocopies of articles to give to Marie Laurance Lassegue.

Then, we arrived at 10:00 a.m. at her office. She made us wait until 11:00, and then introduced us to her cabinet director, whose role was to hear what we needed and write a report to her; then and she would do the follow-up if need be. I explained to her briefly that I needed the Minister of Culture's support for a new performing arts center that I wanted to build in Port-au-Prince, and I also needed their support in helping in the cleaning process at The New Victorian School. She promised to submit the report and we left. Of course, we never received any response from her.

In the meantime, the crisis of the maid, who had been discovered for over twenty-four hours, had been exacerbated. Her body was not only decomposing, but during the night, the dogs ate part of her feet. Thus, she had to go as soon as possible and it couldn't wait until we found my wife so that they could go together. So I went to the school, called the family, and they came to get her. The coffin which I had built the previous afternoon was ready. So, at around 2:00, two members of the family, the uncle and the brother, went to the body and put in in the coffin. All the workers and other people in the yard ran away because of the foul smell. I never smelled anything like it before. So I also left the yard. They took the body out. They put it on a truck and took it to the cemetery. It's amazing how scared people were of dead body and the power of the spirit of the dead person.

On Day 10, April 7th, I had to get up really early, around 5:00 a.m., because I had to meet with the parents of The New Victorian School students. It was a short meeting, where I informed them that our goal was to start school on May 10th 2010, and we would work until August 20th. We also discussed monthly tuition and other details. Following the meeting, I virtually stayed in the school, watching the workers working, hoping that they would have found Myslie. But by the end of the day, they still hadn't reached her yet. I was somewhat disappointed, but I was hoping tomorrow would be a better day. I really wanted Myslie to be found in order to close this chapter and to move on.

I also needed this episode of my life to be over because Myslie's family was not as caring and loving to her as they used to seem when she was alive. Their behavior fit the new Haitian expression:"zo-blood," which means "don't care." They really didn't care about her. All they needed was to see what she had that they could take.

April 9th was the day that we were sure that Myslie was going to be found. As I wrote earlier, on the day of the earthquake, I asked Myslie to come upstairs to the third floor with me to find Onickel so that we could fix the Internet connection. She wanted to stay in our apartment instead, and read. "I'll be right back," were the last words I said to her. I'd taken almost three months to keep that promise, but by April 8th, we still hadn't found Myslie even though the workers had reached the pile of concrete where our apartment had been. I couldn't go up on the big mound of rubble because of my wheelchair, but Victoria did, and she took pictures and told me what she saw.

On April 9th, we got up again at approximately the same time, around 5:30 in the morning, and we were at the school by 7:30. The workers were finally in our room. I was excited. Much of my computer hardware was found, though we had to take it to a computer repair specialist to back up the information on it. Unfortunately, only three of twenty computers could be saved. I was getting increasingly frustrated because Josette, Myslie's sister, was busy taking materials that belonged to the school because she believed they were Myslie's.

We were able to find many school books, music books, CDs, videos, and even bottles of drinks that weren't broken, etc. But there was no strange smell. It was as if Myslie wasn't there. I was wondering what was going on. Did she have time to run out to the street and die out there? But finally by around 1:00 p.m., the workers saw a foot. It was Myslie's foot. Victoria came and gave me the news. She was found. At once, I called the driver who was supposed to take her to the cemetary. I also called my good friend Rev. David Cesar, who is an Episcopalian priest, orchestra conductor, and violist.

They carefully broke the surrounding cement. Myslie was on the bed, face down, under a slab of roof. Apparently, right after I went upstairs, she lay down on the bed. Usually, when she only napped, she put the pillows against the wall and lay across the bed, her feet hanging over the edge. This time, we think she may have been sleeping on her side,in the normal night sleeping position, with her head facing the bathroom, as someone seven months pregnant might sleep – on her side, We found her on her stomach probably because of the shaking and the pressure of five stories falling on her.

Also, unlike the maid, we smelled almost nothing. Selita had died in a place that allowed air to reach her, and the air caused decomposition, with all the disagreeable odors that went with it. But Myslie was preserved because she was closed in a way where no air could have penetrated to her tomb.

Because we had such a terrible experience with the maid from two days ago with the foul odor, where we all had to run to the streets, I had purchased the necessary items: strong powerful disinfectant, Clorox, and Formol to remove the odor from the body, even incense. But fortunately, Myslie was so well-preserved and protected that the smell wasn't too bad.

From the way she was found, it appeared that she died instantly. However, the fact that her body didn't have any type of marks or cuts or bruises, indicated that she could have been alive for a while before she died. Such a wonderful woman did not deserve such a painful and terrifying death. In fact, no one should have to die that way. But we are not here to judge or decide anyone's fate. Only God can make such a determination.

I did thoroughly enjoy the twenty months, (June 2008 through January 2010) that we dated, and the three months of marriage that we had together. She was a unique individual, and I hope she had a few seconds of life to pray so that she may be in heaven.

The workers put Myslie in the coffin and brought her down through the wreckage to the ground. I stopped them, and they opened the box so I could see her and say goodbye. While she was there, members of her family were very busy, looking into her two purses to see what she left, and her two bank account books to see how much money she left for them.

I had finally had enough of them. I started screaming at them, telling them how horrible and inconsiderate they were. I told them that maybe, God made the right decision by taking her away so that she wouldn't have to deal with such a detestable family.

The driver came, and a few minutes later, Father David came. We quickly had a short but beautiful religious service for her, and she was taken away by her brothers to the cemetery, where she was laid to rest.

The family cried bitterly, mostly because Myslie was the breadwinner. She was the one providing financial support to most of them. Myslie was gone. This life was finally over, and I was ready to move on to whatever my new life had to offer. I felt as if the notorious earthquake episode was over. That part of my life had ended and I was ready to start a new life. I would always miss Myslie, but life would have to go on.

Saturday, April 10th, was a quiet day, which I called a day of resolution. We simply went to the school, trying to save whatever little we could from my bathroom, where there were was much school property that we needed, as well as all my clothes. My violin was found, but inside the case there was water, due to a pipe that broke during the earthquake, and it was all broken up.

On April 11th, which was Sunday, we stayed home all day, Victoria with a horrible cold from staying too long in the dust and sun, and I had a horrible stomachache. My driver and Marie Marthe, an old friend of mine, came to our rescue and brought us medicine.

On Monday April 12th, we went back to work, starting the construction of a depot, which is a small storage house, in order to save all the school materials, because the big old building had to be destroyed due to heavy damage.

Though there was so much work to be done, it was nothing like the emotional pressure of the previous week. It took four days to build the storage space and to move as much as we could into it.

In addition, we had heard from Mr. Benjamin. He accepted my apology and was interested in working on the project of the Haiti Performing Arts Center. We met with him, gave him the preliminary text, and explained to him what our goals were for this project. He promised to start working on it right away. That was an important step, for Mr. Benjamin was not only an architect and engineer, but also an excellent musician. He would be able to understand my musical approach and architectural needs.

Though we went back to the States on April 16th for more doctor's appointments and therapy, we had to make a short trip back to Haiti at the end of April through May 4th in order to prepare for reopening of school on May 10th.

Our students would go to school at another academic institution, the George Marc Institute, from May 10th through August 13th. Though the schedule -- 12:00 p.m. to 4:00 p.m. -- was really difficult for the parents, they were nevertheless happy to have their children in school.

May 6th, however, was a turning point in my medical situation. I went to the hospital in the early morning at 6:00 for three surgeries. Doctor Villela was to remove the iron fixator which had been in my left foot since January 15th, and Doctor Owens had to put in the middle and ring fingers of my left hand a metal plate which would facilitate the healing process of the fingers. He also had to correct a problem which I had in the ring finger of my left hand since before the earthquake, which is called trigger finger. Trigger finger is a condition that affects the tendons in your fingers or thumb. Trigger finger limits finger movement. When you try to straighten your finger, it will lock or catch before popping out straight.

By afternoon, all the surgeries were completed and I had to stay overnight for observation. The experience was more pleasant since I knew what to expect. A special boot was put on my left foot and a cast on my left hand, and I was sent home on the afternoon of May 7th. One week later, Doctor Owens substituted the cast I had with a removable one, and Doctor Vilella did the same for my left foot.

I was truly happy to see the iron fixator gone and I felt more like a normal human being.

My next appointments with both doctors were for June 2nd with Doctor Owens, and June 4th with Doctor Vilella. In the meantime, I had to go to therapy. I also took daily walks and did exercises in my room. I was steadily improving. The pain in my feet and left hand had gradually abated to a tolerable level which allowed me to rarely take the horrible pain medicine.

During these resting days, I was able to work on the preliminary steps of my new dream project which was the construction of the Haiti Performing Arts Center, or HPAC. I sent out the necessary application to the Florida Division of the Secretary of State to legalize the new international institution I had created, named Friends of Music Education for Haiti, Inc. or FMEH, which would manage the Haiti Performing Arts Center.

THE MIRACLE OF MUSIC

HAITI PERFORMING ARTS CENTER

The mission of Friends of Music Education for Haiti, Inc. is to contribute to the overall development of music education and performance opportunities for children, youth, and interested adults, to help initiate musical training in all private and public schools throughout the country, to explore Haiti's rich traditional music, to actively participate in fundraising for its different projects, and to manage the construction of the Haiti Performing Arts Center.

In June 2010, I did receive the official legal documents from the state, recognizing FMEH as a non profit organization. At once, I applied to the Internal Revenue Service for a 501(c)(3) tax exempt status, which was approved on August 6th, 2010.

I was also carefully selecting the people that I wanted to be on the first board of Directors of FMEH. This selection process was very difficult, for they had to be a diverse group of individuals based on their sex, race, religion, and professions, and they had to be interested in music education and Haiti.

The month of May was also emotionally draining. I was really missing Myslie, especially on my birthday (May 19th). Somehow, I couldn't believe that she was gone and she would never come back. When I married her, I was really hoping that she would be the last woman I would have for the rest of my life, and now she was gone; never to return. As it is written in the book: (Savinien de Cyrano de Bergerac, March 1619/July 28th 1665) "Mourir n'est pas terrible, mais ne plus la revoir jamais, voilà l'horrible." That is: "Dying is not terrible; but to never see her again is horrible."

I cried constantly, wondering if I would ever find a woman like Myslie again. I tried to think that it was God's decision to take her away from me for whatever reason, and he would surely give me another one in time.

On Friday June 4th 2010, Victoria and I were on the road again. This time to Hartford, Connecticut, for a benefit concert entitled: "Song of Haiti for the reconstruction of The New Victorian School." It was organized by members of the "Song for Haiti Committee" who heard the story of my situation and the destruction of the New Victorian School on NPR, National Public Radio.

The concert took place on Sunday June 6th at 5:00 p.m. Though it was preceded by a big thunderstorm, over 1000 people attended the event. The performance included members of the Hartford and New Haven Symphony Orchestras, and a 150-member choir. The centerpiece of the concert was the final movement of Beethoven's Symphony No. 9. Other works on the program included Mozart's "Ave Verum Corpus," a choral transcription of the *Largo* from Dvorak's Symphony No. 9, Randall Thompson's "Alleluia," a work for organ and brass, and an interfaith hymn.

The concert was extraordinary, though I cried once they

played "Ave Verum Corpus" by Mozart because it was on a CD that Myslie played the night of January 11th. I had prepared this CD for her so she would listen to it every night while falling asleep, because as it is believed by the theory of the Mozart effect, the baby who was seven months old, would have his little brain stimulated by listening to Mozart's music.

During the concert, a proclamation was read where June the 6th was proclaimed by the governor of the state, Governor Rell, to be "Romel Joseph Day." That was truly amazing. I also gave a short speech, thanking everyone for their unreserved support and generosity.

We came back to Miami on June 7th, and on June 8th, I went back -- this time by myself -- to Haiti to start working on the reconstruction process. It was going to be a very busy but also a relaxing time. On June 10th, I completed the BBC report, where about 150 of our returning students presented a short welcome program and I played the violin for them. My playing didn't sound great but everyone was happy the fact that I was able to play the violin again.

On June 11th, the World Cup soccer started. Everyone in Haiti was excited. There were at least two games per day and due to the games, we had lots of electricity, which was fantastic. My team was Argentina, but most people in Haiti were for Brazil. They were really unhappy toward the end of the tournament because both Argentina and Brazil were eliminated.

Since April 2010, I have been working on rebuilding The New Victorian School. The reconstruction is in three stages:

1. The demolition of the old building which was severely damaged, the buildings and removal of all rubble,

2. The construction of a temporary shelter in order for school to start on September 13th, 2010.

3. The permanent reconstruction of the academic section of The New Victorian School, and its expanded music section, which will become "The New Haiti Performing Arts Center."

On July 20th, 2010, we began the construction of the temporary shelter, which constituted phase two of the reconstruction process. Part of the shelter's construction ended on September 12th, just in time for school to start on September 13th. If all goes well, we expect the complete temporary shelter to be finished by December 2010. The classrooms are very crowded and the office area is limited in space for the administrative staff.

In contrast to past years, we didn't have many students, particularly the two- or three-year-olds, crying on their first day of school. They were all excited and happy to be back in class. We are all looking forward to a great 2010-2011 school year.

Beginning January 12th, 2011, the first anniversary of the earthquake, The New Victorian School will begin Phase Three of the reconstruction process. This includes both the academic and music section.

Just as before the earthquake, the academic section has an English component which uses a Christian American curriculum from second to twelfth grade, and a French section from ages two to "Philo," the last grade in the Haitian curriculum. The French section uses the curriculum of the National Education in Haiti.

The music section has been expanded to become the first **"Haiti Performing Arts Center."** The goals of Haiti Performing Art Center are:

1. To build a concert hall capable of holding 1200 attendees, with a state of the art stage, including an orchestra

pit in order for different types of performances such as symphony orchestras, chamber music, opera, ballet, and musical theater to take place, with a balcony above the stage for choirs. The concert hall will also contain dividers which will make it possible to present smaller-scale concerts and recitals to a limited number of attendees. In addition, the Haiti Performing Art Center will contain office space, dressing rooms, a lobby with a box office, a reception hall, a loading dock, audience and performers' restrooms, a sound control/recording room, a lighting control booth, and a mechanical room for electrical, air conditioning, and other equipment.

Moreover, it will be accessible for people with disabilities; which includes accessible seating in the hall, elevators, ramps, handrails for the stairs, a handicapped bathroom, accessible door width, Braille character signage, and door protective and reopening devices.

2. To construct a music conservatory building which will have school administration office space, a special room for ballet classes, one large room for music theater, one large room for group keyboard lessons, two studios for piano, two studios for violin, one for viola, one for cello, one for bass; four small rooms for woodwind, four rooms for brass, one medium-sized room for percussion, two large rooms for miscellaneous rehearsal groups (such as for the youth orchestra), a school library, an instrument repair and storage room, a store for instrument parts, sheet music, and other articles, a small café/restaurant, a computer lab, a sound recording instructional room for sound

engineering classes, a room for videography classes, and bathrooms -- and all must be handicapped accessible.

3. Permanent resident staff quarters where long-term international contracted instructors and volunteers can live. This building will contain apartment-like rooms, in the form of a suite. Each room will have a small living room space, a small kitchen, and a bedroom/bathroom suite.

4. A smaller building which contains a generator, inverters, and batteries to ensure that all buildings always have electricity.

5. To initiate all children, youth, and interested adults into a musical instrument as well as the rudiments of music in order to build a large audience who can appreciate quality performances, and to prepare amateur as well as professional musicians.

6. To train new music instructors through a professional development program in order to have more music teachers in all Haiti's private and public elementary, middle, and high schools.

7. Working in collaboration with reputable musical institutions and professional musicians around the world in order to equip the students with valuable musical knowledge, instrumental training, and numerous possibilities to perform as orchestra members and soloists, as well as becoming concert attendees.

8. To put in place an international exchange program between students of the conservatory and those abroad.

9. To create the first Haiti Symphony Orchestra, "HSO," which will composed of professional Haitian musicians and those from other countries.

10. To encourage the establishment of youth orchestras through out the country.

The need for the Haiti Performing Arts Center is of the utmost importance to the cultural development of the new Haiti. The essence of our music education and performance program is based on the belief that musical studies can play a significant role in student academic education and in lifelong learning, as well as their social, emotional, and psychological development. Our philosophy is strongly supported by numerous research, notably "The Mozart Effect" by Don Campbell and Associates, which demonstrates that unborn babies listening to orchestral or classical music, especially Mozart's compositions, through their mother's womb during pregnancy and childhood years, do better academically as children and youth than those that do not. In addition, according to The American Music Conference, 52% of music-makers are more likely to go on to college and other higher education than non-music-makers.

The benefits of music education and performance opportunities are enormous for Haiti's children and youth. Many of the essential skills needed in order to create an excellent community are found in studying music, such as: self-esteem, self-confidence, academic performance, and excellent memory. In addition, it's a creative outlet for self-expression, it encourages teamwork, develops structure and a sense of organization and discipline, and brings people together.

Furthermore, the earthquake was one of the most dramatic moments for all children and adults who experienced it, and it will have a permanent effect on the psychological and emotional stability of these citizens. Music studies and performance opportunities can serve as an excellent vehicle to reduce the negative effects of the earthquake on the Haitian society.

Building the first Performing Arts Center in Haiti during the post-earthquake era, is a supremely challenging task. Many people believe that food, water, and medical care are all that are needed by the Haitian population, and the arts, culture and social activities should take a back seat. However, I believe that it is indispensable that music, particularly music education and instrumental training, as well as performances, must be included and integrated into the cultural fabric of Haiti.

Though this is a highly challenging project, with the help and support of all my friends, and all those interested in promoting music education for children and youth, we will succeed, for Haiti is in desperate need of academic education, as well as music education and instrumental training for children and youth.

I consider myself to have a truly rich and interesting life, full of happy and unhappy times. I was able to successfully use my Christian faith, as well as music, particularly the violin, to overcome many challenges throughout my life. In addition, I was determined to make as many of my childhood dreams come true as possible, by using what I call "**The ten keys to ultimate success**," and they are:

1. **Have your dream.** A dream is an idea. Your role is to make this dream materialize.

2. **Have faith in yourself.** You must have confidence in your abilities. You must believe that you will achieve your dream even when you are faced with insurmountable obstacles which could prevent your dream from coming true.

3. **Work hard.** Do all that is necessary, day and night, in order for your dream to become reality.

4. **Have patience.** Be persistent. Try not to get frustrated or discouraged when things are not working according to plan. Make the factor of time your greatest friend. To the question: "When?" your answer should be: "For as long as it takes."

5. **Constant determination.** Press ahead; move steadily toward achieving each goal which will bring you to your ultimate desire.

6. **Imagination.** Try to come up with ideas that will bring you closer to your dream. Imagination answers the question "What? What can I do to move from step (A) to step (B)?"

7. Creativity. You need to come up with ways to implement the ideas which come from your imagination. Creativity answers the question "How? How can I make this idea work?"

8. **The courage to accept rejection from others.** That's a hard one. Accept rejection with grace, and keep asking until you receive what you need; for it is written: "Ask and you shall receive."

9. **Learn from your mistakes and move forward.** Remember, you can make one million mistakes and that's okay; but

you must not make the same mistake twice if you can help it, for all actions have negative or positive consequences.

10. And most importantly, seek the support of your family, friends and community. **Just never give up!**

My mission for the rest of my life is to help ensure that music education is included in the curricula of elementary and high schools in Haiti, that children are able to play to a certain level on a chosen musical instrument, that Haiti has a state of the art concert hall where professional and non-professional musicians can perform, a conservatory where professional musicians can be trained, and a professional Haiti Symphony Orchestra as a lasting legacy and heritage to this suffering yet wonderful country.

Please join me, and let's move together toward improving the lives of the children and youth of Haiti through academic education, as well as music education and instrumental training.

References

ARTICLES:

Out of "a grave," Haitian violinist keeps music in his heart. By Michael Sallah, Miami Herald.
http://www.miamiherald.com/news/southflorida/v-fullstory/story/1436927.html?storylink=fbuser

South Miami Middle School Chamber Ensemble plays for Haitian violinist, Romel Joseph, at Jackson Memorial Hospital. By Hannah Sampson, Miami Herald.
http://www.miamiherald.com/haiti/help-and-healing/story/1441002.html

Trapped violinist found deliverance through prayers, concertos, CNN
http://edition.cnn.com/2010/WORLD/americas/01/27/haiti.violinist/

Stevie Wonder to give keyboards to violinist quake survivor, Romel Joseph, Miami Herald
http://www.miamiherald.com/2010/01/28/1450073/stevie-wonder-to-give-keyboards.html

Miami Symphony Orchestra helps Haitian Musician, WSVN
http://www.wsvn.com/news/articles/local/MI144245/

Earthquake survivor and violinist plans return to Haiti, Miami Herald
http://www.miamiherald.com/2010/03/13/1527324/violinist-romel-joseph-gets-ready.html

Romel Joseph returns to quake-hit Haiti to rebuild his New Victorian School – again, by Martin Fletcher, The Times UK
http://www.timesonline.co.uk/tol/news/world/us_and_americas/article7085153.ece#comment-have-your-say

Blind Violinist Struggles To Rebuilt Haiti In His Own Way
http://www.palmbeachpost.com/news/world/blind-violinist-struggles-to-rebuild-haiti-in-his-803970.html

VIDEOS:

Haitian violinist tells story of survival. By Emily Michot, Miami Herald.
http://www.miamiherald.com/video/index.html?media_id=9520080

THE MIRACLE OF MUSIC

A Tale of Two Tragedies. CBS Interview with Katie Couric.
   http://www.cbsnews.com/video/watch/?id=6126869n

A Special Visit to Romel Joseph. By Hector Gabino, Miami
   Herald.
   http://www.miamiherald.com/video/index.html?media_
   id=9577208

Music Heals Blind Violinist, CNN courtesy of WSVN
   http://www.cnn.com/video/data/2.0/video/
   world/2010/01/25/dnt.haiti.violinist.healing.wsvn.html

Symphony In The Rubble by John Zarrella, CNN
   http://www.cnn.com/video/data/2.0/video/
   world/2010/01/27/zarrella.violinist.survivor.cnn.html

Pledging To Play Again – Surprise gift from Stevie Wonder by
   Kyra Phillips, CNN.
   http://www.cnn.com/video/data/2.0/video/
   world/2010/01/27/nr.intv.joseph.wonder.violin.cnn.html

Quake Survivor Plays Again, John Zarrella, CNN
   http://www.cnn.com/video/data/2.0/video/
   world/2010/02/17/zarrella.haiti.violinist.gift.cnn.html

Blind Violinist Recovering, John Zarrella, CNN
   http://www.cnn.com/video/data/2.0/video/
   living/2010/03/15/haiti.blind.violinist.update.cnn.html

ROMEL JOSEPH

Quake violinists hands, faith heal, CNN
  http://www.cnn.com/video/data/2.0/video/
  world/2010/07/12/nr.int.romel.joseph.haiti.cnn.html

RADIO:

Wife, School Lost In Haiti Quake, Blind Violinist Vows To
  Rebuild : NPR
  http://www.npr.org/templates/story/story.
  php?storyId=122900781

LaVergne, TN USA
05 January 2011
211091LV00009B/7/P